EOT CHART

ADVANCEMENT STEPS

EXECUTIVE CONSIDERATIONS	EXPOSE CONDITIONS	DEVELOP IDEAS	UNIFY VIEWS	DETERMINE PLANS	PRODUCE ACTIONS	REVIEW RESULTS
1. IDENTIFY SUBJECTS	Expose conditions by identifying subjects; e.g., through Collecting Sources					
2. EXPRESS PARTICULARS		Develop ideas by expressing particulars; e.g., through Suggesting Recommendations				
3. ANALYZE RELATIONS			Unify views by analyzing relations; e.g., through Mediating Group Opinions			
4. COORDINATE PURPOSES				Determine plans by coordinating purposes; e.g., through Foreseeing Strategies		
5. CONTROL CERTAINTIES					Produce actions by controlling certainties; e.g., through Emphasizing Advancements	
6. EVALUATE SATISFACTIONS						Review results by evaluating satisfactions; e.g., through Weighing Improvements

An Executive

Operations Technique

C. DON WILLIAMSON

Founder,
Williamson-Dickie Manufacturing Company

An Executive

Operations Technique

PRENTICE-HALL, INC.

Englewood Cliffs, New Jersey

1963

An Executive Operations Technique
C. Don Williamson

Revised and Enlarged Edition

PRENTICE-HALL INTERNATIONAL, INC., *London*
PRENTICE-HALL OF AUSTRALIA, PTY., LTD., *Sydney*
PRENTICE-HALL OF CANADA, LTD., *Toronto*
PRENTICE-HALL FRANCE, S.A.R.L., *Paris*
PRENTICE-HALL OF JAPAN, INC., *Tokyo*
PRENTICE-HALL DE MEXICO, S.A., *Mexico City*

Library of Congress Catalog Card Number: 63-9964

Printed in the United States of America
29421—C

Foreword

From years of executive experience, C. Don Williamson formulated a set of very powerful concepts to be used as executive tools. His ideas are powerful because of their soundness and simplicity; the communication of them is complicated because of the infinite complexity of life in which they are used.

Before one begins to study the exposition of EOT, therefore, it may be useful to check some preliminary bench marks. My purpose is not to attempt a summary, but to see if I can indicate some useful expectations of what a reader might look for and how the concepts and experience might be used.

For more than twelve years it was my privilege to work with Mr. Williamson and his associates at Williamson-Dickie in his dedicated effort to distill the essential concepts which could be carried over from one situation to another. In all those years, only the initials EOT were used, their meaning having long since run beyond the words of the book title, which now appear to have somewhat surprising limitations.

As Mr. Williamson explained in his Introduction to EOT, it was his curiosity about the questions executives asked which started him on the research from which EOT grew. His interest in questions struck a common chord with me at our first meeting, because Dr. Melvin T. Copeland and I had just finished research on *The Board of Directors and Business Management*, in which we found that one of the major qualifications of a good director was his skill in "Asking Discerning Questions." Mr. Williamson and I could agree that questions were the connecting link between generalizations which had emerged from experience and the particulars of each individual situation which an executive had to handle. We never could quite agree on the type of generalization, concept, or model which best promoted these connecting link questions. Perhaps it was the persistence of a somewhat different orientation, along with a common interest in effective dealing with specific cases, which always made our discussions seem mutually stimulating.

I think it would be fair to say that, as the responsible head of an enterprise, Mr. Williamson felt the need for a procedural model that could not only raise discerning questions, but also get them answered. He had been working toward an inclusive system of concepts under which all executive

v

experience could be classified. These concepts and experiences are useful in meeting new problems by guiding executives to questions which will be most fruitful.

Since most men are working in existing organizations, it seems generally more useful to start with the application of EOT to the task of living in a structure rather than to the task of building a new one. One's position in the organization, therefore, becomes a prime reference in the use of EOT and the discussion of concrete events in terms of EOT concepts. What may be the result of a staff executive's research may become only one of many conditions in a situation facing a senior executive. Alertness to this difference in reference by both executives will enable them to discuss the situation with better understanding and more discerning questions.

Some incidents can be handled at once. Others lead to undertakings which require more time or more collateral developments than are immediately available. The executive increases his contribution to the company by pulling out from the stream of things for which he is responsible such projects or *items* to keep on his agenda for systematic attention and scheduled advancement. These critical incidents and items come to the executive's attention in four major ways: (a) from his senior executives; (b) from his staff associates; (c) from his subordinates; and (d) from his own judgment of what the situation requires. This last ability to initiate significant items is of the greatest importance to the progress of the company (assuming, of course, an attendant ability to schedule the item on through to positive results). Development of this ability is one of the key objectives of professional executive development.

One purpose of EOT is to provide a pattern against which to compare situations so as to reveal opportunities. When lost at sea, the navigator gets his bearings by chronometer and sextant; or, now, by tuning his directional antenna on two different radio stations and plotting the intersection. The EOT pattern of concepts helps to answer the question of what to do next by helping an executive locate himself: first in relation to the advancement of the item; and second in relation to the levels of executive consideration required.

The basic concept of EOT is that items advance through a sequence. Conditions must be exposed from which ideas can be developed. Around these, views are unified so that a plan can be determined. Then action must be produced so that results can be reviewed for side effects and new opportunities.

Events do not take this happy course without skilled consideration by the executive of the subjects which he has identified to the point where he can express them in such particulars as costs, ratios, and positions. Analysis of how the elements in the situation are related leads to consideration of purposes and how they may be coordinated, and adequate controls established for the uncertainties predicted. Throughout, the executive is evaluating the situation being moved by the dissatisfaction he feels or the level of satisfaction he demands.

An item advances only as the executive brings skillful consideration to bear at each step. And, as the item does advance, new developments emerge which require reconsideration. There is a continuous process of interaction between advancement of the item by consideration and the generation of new considerations through advancement. The experience from which the EOT pattern derives indicates that speed is not gained by skipping steps in the advancement process, but by increased skill in dealing with the necessary levels of consideration.

Even though he becomes oriented to the current advancement of the situation and the level of consideration required, an executive may still not know what to do. It is for this event that Mr. Williamson wrote the EOT text. It is the accumulation of his lifetime of executive experience organized in terms of action suggestions.

Identification of the level at which the item needs consideration can also suggest the kind of expert help to call on, or point to an area in which the executive may want to do some personal development. The difference in ability to handle different considerations is one of the major facts taken into account by management in matching men and executive jobs. Use of EOT as a search pattern may thus help in executive selection and organization. At Williamson-Dickie Manufacturing Company, the same findings have been the basis for designing an intensive executive development program.

The executive is an artist as well as a scientist. Unlike the engineer who has injected controlled amounts of fuel and air before lighting a spark, the executive is dealing with other men whose free choices may upset the most careful predictions. The EOT pattern of concepts takes this powerful force of free will into account and helps the executive carry his responsibilities of creative leadership.

No one will be less satisfied with the book than Mr. Williamson would have been himself. He was taken away when the white-up was still largely at the glossary or encyclopedia stage, while points were unevenly developed. He had visualized that the planned discussions of experiences from within the executive group during the next year would provide much more illustrative material and demonstrate more clearly the ways in which EOT could be used. The perfectionism which drove him on was moderated by his executive experience of using what was available. Posthumous publication of the book in its present stage, therefore, is consistent with his practice of step by step refinement, and his desire to have others participate in its evolution.

Fortunately for others, this version of his thinking about EOT can make a significant contribution to a wide range of readers. To the practicing executive the utility of his experience will be immediately grasped. For those who are concerned with the emergence of management as a profession, here is a pioneer who began forty years ago to think of himself as an executive, to identify himself with management as a profession. Although he owned the business, his concern with profits was not so much a return on investment as a measure of his success as an executive. In a business which economists might consider in terms of buying and selling cotton cloth, he skillfully performed the functions of the merchant but thought of himself as an executive. Surviving in a highly competitive industry by engineering continuous improvements in plant, product, and processes, he was an engineer but spoke of himself as an executive.

Copy for this book came to me in India, where I was completing a year and a half assignment to help with a management development program. I cannot stress enough the importance of this personal identification with management as a profession. In the so-called developing economies, some enterprises have produced fabulous profits in the past. The great need is the concept of management as a profession. Mr. Williamson's competitors will testify that his interest in being a good executive in no way dulled the thrust of his enterprise. For executives and others who parted company with him over the years, there may well be continuing differences of opinion. I think even they would agree that to a rare degree among men, Mr. Williamson had disciplined himself to think of the situation and to respond to its requirements; to accept criticisim and suggestions as contributions to the situation rather than as personal attacks. For associates who struggled with him in the evolution of EOT, there has been growth and development. For his friends, there always will be the wonder of how one who always responded so generously and actively ever found time to record so much of his professional interest in becoming a better executive.

ANDREW R. TOWL

Director of Case Development
Graduate School of Business Administration
Harvard University
Boston, Massachusetts

Preface

Effective operations at Williamson-Dickie Manufacturing Company come in good measure from our management's use of what we call Executive Operations Technique. Throughout my business career I have observed new executives gaining maturity of judgment and effectiveness by applying these Executive Operations Techniques. Now that the company's growth is bringing more men and women into our executive group, a more complete statement of EOT should be made available.

How to start such a statement is puzzling. After several attempts, there seems to be no better way than to start at the beginning. I hesitate to do this, because EOT is now a well organized group effort of about fifty executives. Our early struggles, however, may lend encouragement to those who are getting into EOT for the first time.

Looking back on the years of developmental effort at Williamson-Dickie devoted to identifying executive fundamentals, we may be encouraged by the significant improvement to be seen. The early attempts were halting, groping efforts that often seemed to confuse one thing while they clarified another. Semantic difficulties have always been severe; finding words that convey precise abstract meanings often has meant an exhaustive search. Terminology and theoretical patterns are still flexible, and the reader is still urged to offer alternative expressions and concepts.

By 1921, on the threshold of my executive career, I was convinced that a system of guiding generalizations was useful in virtually any endeavor undertaken. In my five years at college, courses were typically presented as a group or system of "principles" or "fundamentals." Even football and boxing were analyzed and taught in this manner. It appeared that almost every skill made use of these guiding generalizations to remind, to simplify, and to help the individual work such skills into the intuitive pattern of his performance.

College courses in business management were exceedingly rare in the 1920's, however, and little aid could be secured from that source. The "scientific management" movement was still in its infancy, with only scant attention being paid to the problems of general management and executive activity. Some management books appearing in that day were helpful in limited areas of business activity, but their scope was usually too narrow for them to be generally useful. The popular books on executive operations, emphasizing "self-help" and moralistic advice on conduct, were distinctly lacking in analytical and operational utility.

As a consequence, my early efforts to identify executive fundamentals were to a great extent pioneering into an uncharted area. After surviving the depressions of 1920 and 1929, I was convinced that static bromides were of little value as guidance clues in executive situations. By 1935, the search for fundamentals had become an intensive one. I felt that I needed every aid possible to improve my technique as an executive. And I knew that mastery and reliance on a few more or less proved fundamentals would carry the firm through any subsequent crisis that might arise. Furthermore, I began to sense the need for developing more effective managers in the Williamson-Dickie organization.

In the early stages of this effort, the "principles" we identified were often static. They were "do's and don'ts," which if useful at all only aided a backward-looking review. They did not stimulate typically effective executive responses. Generally they related to what things and people *are* rather than to what things and people *do*. Not being behavioristic, they failed to suggest positive actions directed toward a realistic goal.

Realizing the importance of *ideas* in creative executive operations, we started emphasizing this approach to operating problems. Later it became clear, however, that the use of a more inductive approach produced better results. After a careful study of the factual conditions, useful ideas seemed to occur spontaneously. Sometimes our executive group overemphasized this inductive approach, however, resulting in loss of time and effort that might have been saved by a more extensive use of deduction.

One of the most productive approaches we used in these earlier developmental years was the collection and analysis of questions asked in executive conferences. We found that questioning was one of the most obvious ways by which executive behavior was displayed. In questioning, an executive usually has a particular purpose in mind; in most cases, facts are being sought. More specifically, conditions that influence the success or failure of an executive undertaking are exposed.

Altogether we collected several thousand questions asked in business conferences. Then we began studying them for clues to possible categories that these questions might be grouped within. It did not take long to develop generalizations in rudimentary form.

Thus a number of "Performance Factors" were inferred from these generalizations. Twenty-one of these "Performance Factors" were set forth in 1942 in a seven-page pamphlet entitled, "FIP-Sequence of Getting Things Done." These factors were divided into three groups of seven. In the first group, called the Performance Cycle, were placed Facts, Ideas, Plan, Judgment, and Action; when the work was delegated, two other factors—Salesmanship and Supervision—were also brought into play. A second group of seven factors were to be utilized in "increasing the number of items handled by individuals within a cooperative group." They were Time, Method, Organization, Personnel, Personal Balance, Emphasis, and Economy. The third group of factors were "Considerations" to be viewed and included Schedule, Results, Activity, Problem, Similarity, Value, and Accuracy.

Our top executives met weekly to discuss actual business problems and to test by discussion and application the logical soundness of these Performance Factors. One of the difficulties encountered at this stage was the need to sustain continuity in these discussions between the case material and the Performance Factors. Needless to say, we ran into many logical inconsistencies. Some of the consulting advisers, after observing the meetings, remarked that our system had too many "whiskers." Often, we ruefully agreed.

One thing seemed to be true: when new terminology was introduced or when fresh logical relationships were adopted, these improvements made the pattern fall more in line with habitual executive behavior. Exposure of logical inconsistencies in the EOT structure, then, has had salutary effects. Little need has ever been found to reverse the course of improvements and return to former terminology.

The progressive changes in the number and wording of these first Performance Factors and their evolution up to the present are shown in Figure 1. By 1946, the number of factors had been reduced to 18 from the original 21 first introduced in 1942. The number was further reduced to 12 by 1950, and there it has remained since, even though wording had continued to change somewhat. The most significant change in wording evolved from Dr. Carroll L. Shartle's suggestion that the meaning of the factors would be more easily understood if each consisted of a verb-noun phrase. During their evolutionary sequence, the principal factors in the EOT pattern were successively called Performance Factors, Activators, Guide Points, and now, Emphasis Areas.

About 1953, we began trying to catalogue the many specific tools and techniques used by executives in operating situations. This effort resulted in the compilation of 144 guide points summarized in the body of the EOT Chart. Relations among these guide points and the emphasis areas that they are located within have been carefully examined and revised since 1953, resulting in more logical groupings within the chart. Also, some guide points have been consolidated with others and new guide points have been added.

Earlier Editions of EOT

From its first printing in 1942, the concept of EOT has expanded through several editions. The 1946 revision was 81 pages long—about twelve times the length of the original edition. Successive revisions following this—in 1951, 1953, 1958, and the present—trace the full growth and development of those earliest concepts.

The expansion was planned, not haphazard. Each edition has trimmed, distilled, condensed, and refined the ideas contained in its predecessor. Meanwhile, significant additions have been discussed, tested, and written up with great care. Even now, more cases illustrating EOT in action are being readied for integration into the next version of this text.

Development of EOT by no means has been a one-man project. Quite to the contrary, we have had the active effort of the fifty or more executives who have helped refine EOT by practicing the concepts in the operation of Williamson-Dickie Manufacturing Company. We also have sought and used the guidance and active service of the best men we could find in the management field. At least a dozen nationally known business consultants and educators have had an influential or active part in the program. They include:

Mr. Edwin J. Booz (deceased), Booz, Allen, and Hamilton, Chicago, Illinois;

Dr. Eliot D. Chapple, cultural anthropologist, The Chapple Company, Noroton, Connecticut;

Mr. Michael J. Kane, business management consultant and President, Training Within Industry Foundation, Boston; former Training Director of the American Telephone and Telegraph Company; former executive of the Training Within Industry Section of the War Production Board (World War II);

Dr. Chester F. Lay, Professor of Management, Southern Methodist University, Dallas, Texas;

Dr. Richard F. Schultz, Counselor on Industrial Relations Methods, New York; former industrial psychologist for the Psychological Corporation;

Dr. Carroll L. Shartle, Professor of Psychology and director of a leadership study project, The Ohio State University, Columbus, Ohio;

Dr. William R. Spriegel, Dean of the College of Business Administration, The University of Texas, Austin, Texas;

Professor Andrew R. Towl, Director of Case Development, Harvard Graduate School of Business Administration, Boston, Massachusetts;

Mr. Harry K. Werst, former partner of Booz, Allen, and Hamilton, and now Operations Vice-President of Williamson-Dickie Manufacturing Company;

Mr. Percival White, Market Analysis and Research Consultant, New York;

Dr. Stanley Allen Self, Associate Professor of Management, North Texas State College, Denton.

In addition to Mr. Werst, Dr. Self and Mr. Towl are currently active in the program. Both make regular visits to Williamson-Dickie headquarters in Fort Worth to attend and conduct EOT conferences and to counsel concerning the program.

Mr. Towl receives a full transcript of the EOT Conferences for study and analysis. His reports and advice on these conferences provide materials for future conferences. I believe that, without his counsel in writing this text, it would have taken many more years for the program to advance to its present point.

The late Mr. Booz, a management specialist who became associated with

THE PROGRESSIVE DEVELOPMENT OF THE EOT EMPHASIS AREAS

1942	1946	1950	1954	1961
Problem	Conditions-Cause	Conditions	Expose Conditions	Expose Conditions
Facts	Facts	Facts		
Ideas	Ideas	Ideas	Develop Ideas	Develop Ideas
Salesmanship	Responsithority		Unify Views	Unify Views
Personal Balance				
Plans	Plans	Plans	Determine Plans	Determine Plans
Method				
Action	Action	Action	Produce Actions	Produce Actions
Supervision	Experience			
Results	Results Control	Results Control	Review Results	Review Results
	Consequences			
	Progress Status			
Similarity	Identity	Identity	Identify Subjects	Identify Subjects
Activity	Inventory-Activity	Figures	Formulate Expressions	Express Particulars
Personnel	Relations	Relations	Analyze Relations	Analyze Relations
Organization				
Schedule	Schedule	Schedule	Coordinate Time	Coordinate Purposes
Time				
Accuracy	Certainty	Certainty	Control Certainties	Control Certainties
Judgment				
Value	Value	Value	Evaluate Satisfactions	Evaluate Satisfactions
Economy				
Emphasis				
	Satisfaction			

FIGURE 1.

the program in 1938, was the first consultant to influence the development of EOT. His six years of working closely with Williamson-Dickie on the project helped to refine the patterns of EOT terminology.

From 1944 to 1946, Mr. Kane conducted many of the regular weekly EOT sessions in Fort Worth, suggested some helpful changes in the EOT pattern, and edited the 1946 publication.

Dr. Schultz advised on EOT from the psychological point of view, which we felt had not been emphasized sufficiently, made independent studies related to the EOT effort, and sent us his findings for examination and use.

Every Saturday morning for two years, Dr. Lay attended the EOT sessions. Three days a week for the same period, he worked to "smooth out" EOT.

Dr. Chapple, a specialist in organization research and a skilled statistician, helped institute statistical methods of judging the skill of EOT participants in identifying concrete examples of executive acts and thought subjects with the various EOT guide points.

Dr. Self, who began attending and conducting EOT Conferences in early 1960, also aided in preparing the present edition for publication.

In 1960, individual conference members developed their own cases for group discussion, thereby learning executive techniques in terms of their own experience.

Other consultants at EOT sessions were Mr. Booz and Dr. Spriegel.

If any one thing has contributed substantially to my own executive point of view, it has been the thirty-five years of frequent contact with experts and authorities who have spent their lifetimes in certain areas of the executive process. They have been able and willing to apply what they have learned to specific business enterprises. I believe that among the best investments this company has ever made has been executive consulting fees.

What we have sought to do in our quest for Executive Operating Techniques has been to isolate and knowingly cultivate the most frequently recurring aspects of executive conduct.

We have not tried to develop new principles of executive operation. We have tried only to discover exactly what fundamentals make and guide successful executives. Our ultimate purpose is to express these fundamentals in usable form. The chapters which follow present a working draft of EOT and a report of its operation to date.

Many of us see further opportunities for clarification and experimentation. Our experience, however, has been that the development of EOT will make more progress if we distribute the present draft in all its roughness than if we hold it up for our own further refinement. We count upon the constructive criticism and case experience of those executives who may be led to test these ideas in their own operations.

FORT WORTH, TEXAS   C. DON WILLIAMSON
JANUARY 1, 1961

Contents

IV

IDENTIFYING SUBJECTS, 29

V

EXPRESSING PARTICULARS, 61

VI

ANALYZING RELATIONS, 85

VII

COORDINATING PURPOSES, 119

VIII

CONTROLLING CERTAINTIES, 149

IX

EVALUATING SATISFACTIONS, 175

X

THE MANAGEMENT CASE IN EXECUTIVE DEVELOPMENT, 203

Illustrations

An Executive

Operations Technique

I

The Pattern
of Executive Operations

What makes an executive? How can one learn to become an executive? These questions have been asked by hundreds of thousands of aspiring men, young and old alike. A number of answers have been provided for these questions perhaps, but they are frequently heavily laden with platitudes. Too often, the instructions are overburdened with moral injunctions concerning "hard work and rigid self-denial" as the ingredients of executive success.

The aspirant, then, is frequently left without a program to follow that is operationally sound. He drifts through his career, working hard and denying himself perhaps, but never really fulfilling his potential for management.

Most businessmen will agree that the right kind of experience will develop executive ability. But experience alone, even though it occurs within a setting calling for the exercise of executive ability, is no guarantee that proper traits and abilities will be developed. It seems clear that properly directed practice will develop ability more effectively than haphazard practice. Furthermore, practice within the outlines of a formal, organized training program is more likely to develop executive ability than incidental experiences alone. Practice sessions combined with the right kind of experience, then, can be highly useful in developing an executive corps within a company.

Many have sought such a program to guide and hasten the development of executives to supplement the expensive and slow "survival of the fittest" methods still used in most companies. The development of competent management personnel can and should be among the primary objectives of every business organization. As such an executive development program progresses, it helps the man and it helps the company.

At Williamson-Dickie, we believe that the individual executive should bear much of the responsibility for self-development. In fact, we recognize that a company-directed effort will be of little value unless the executives participating in the program are strongly motivated personally and are conscientiously seeking to improve their executive skills.

Throughout our quest for techniques to improve executive skills, we have been motivated by the belief that a practicable, understandable code of the fundamentals would achieve two purposes. First, it would create an unexcelled device for accelerating the ripening of junior executives. Second, it would provide an equally practical guide to help senior executives avoid errors in management.

It appears more and more evident that we are not working in a new field but are interpreting natural and universal practices. The methods for successfully solving problems already exist and have been used for centuries. Similarly, many management fundamentals do not change with changing situations.

While it is true that countless executives have the ability to plan and to take decisive action, it is also true that these executives frequently are unconscious of the succession of steps through which they go in carrying a program to its successful conclusion. Having developed their ability over a long period of time, they then act intuitively and habitually. They are often at a loss to explain the origin or sequence of their thoughts and actions. Like the self-taught musician, they "play by ear" and do not find it necessary to read notes.

The musician who cannot read or write musical notation is rarely a successful instructor, although his performances may be popularly successful. He may be able to play melodious, harmonious tunes, but he cannot become a symphony orchestra's conductor. He can communicate only by demonstration. And similarly in the executive situation, instructing subordinates solely by "setting the example" is a notoriously slow and inefficient technique.

In seeking the fundamentals underlying executive operations, we are trying to develop a system of notation to accompany the technique. Successful executives can then function effectively in coaching their subordinates. In this way, the emphasis in executive development is shifted from selection to training and from survival of the fittest to planned progress.

ELEMENTAL BASIS OF THE TECHNIQUE

Some of the main elements in the use of Executive Operations Technique at Williamson-Dickie include the executive, the situation, the undertaken item, the work schedule, the chart of EOT guide points, and the practice sessions.

The Executive

An executive is a person who occupies a position of responsibility in an organization and who formally authorizes and directs the activities of others. He is charged with producing satisfactory results. Executives work with other executives, and the course of individual items of work initiated may be from junior to senior, from colleague to colleague, or from senior to junior. In other words, the lines of communication may be vertical, horizontal, or a combination of both. Many of the terms applied to an "executive" may also be applied to any executive unit, whether it is an integrated management group or an individual.

Coordinated group action by executives is necessary as well as individual executive action, for the hours available to any one individual are severely limited. When the number of items of work undertaken or the scope of the function moves beyond one man's capacity, the responsible executive must multiply the hours of time by arranging for several executives to cooperate in handling the work.

The Situation

Raw material in an executive operation usually exists in the stream of experience, of which the competent executive takes sensitive notice.

He sees before him the present, the oncoming future, and the receding past. His job is to select a workable section of this material which outlines itself to him as a situation. It is this visualization, identification, and expression of a situation that gives the material its tangible, operating form. The executive perceives the situation in terms of his frame of reference and his experience.

The Undertaken Item

Figuratively speaking, the executive's working material may vary in consistency from fluid to solid. This variation of consistency will affect the working characteristics of the material. In fact, this material or information needs to be expressed in some sort of containing vessel or given a particular identity. Different sections may be conveyed by communication, stored for reference, or otherwise handled in processing.

In the EOT pattern, one containing vessel of executive material is called the item. The executive must select from the daily flow of activities for which he is responsible definite items for attention and action. An item thus becomes a unit of executive work, a thing to do, to be scheduled and handled by the executive.

An executive may have ten to twenty such items in his current schedule. The number varies from job to job, from staff to line assignments, and from level to level of supervision.

The carved-out item is not a continuing function or a broad program. It is a small project. It is an undertaken task, with a beginning, a progression, and an end. The lines outlining its scope and suggesting its central meaning are often intuitively drawn; these lines may not be evident until they are put under tension by operating action and receive the stress and attrition brought on by experienced action.

The item undergoes the same progressive development phases as a manufactured product. At what stage the raw material ceases to be a situation and becomes an item is difficult to describe. Executives have definite standards, however, as to when an item reaches its full status of a "job to do."

An item needs to be reduced to action status. Its scope should permit effective and performable action. Action status also implies that an item is in definite shape to be discussed and approved for further attention. The item should also be in an assignable status, although the assignment may be reduced subsequently to a narrower or simpler next step.

Executives with little experience in setting up items sometimes have difficulty selecting a suitable focal scope and may select scopes that are too broad or too narrow. This is influenced more by the customary perspective of the individual than by the nature of his problem.

The process of setting up an item from a situation is discussed in more detail in Chapter IV, under the topic of Undertaking Items. Until then, we shall study the executive operating technique in relation to items already set up.

The Schedule

Executives have made lists of things to do since time immemorial. With such a list an executive can cross off items completed. At the end of the day some items have been completed and crossed off; some may not have been reached; and some may have been started but have not been finished. With the day's work laid out before the executive starts into action, little energy is required to decide what to do. Concentrated emphasis may then be applied to putting the day's work behind him, an objective which in many executive positions becomes a respectable task.

For most executives, however, there are more items than can be dispatched before attention must be turned to the routine and unforeseeable demands of the day. EOT therefore suggests that greatest progress comes from scheduling some time about once a week on all one's items so that none will get lost or delayed by daily pressures. In this way others concerned with the related items may plan their work.

The EOT Chart

In the evolution of EOT, it has been found helpful to represent the pattern of executive operations by means of charts and graphs. These devices serve to aid in visualizing the full scope and meaning of EOT. They compress onto a single page the essential outlines of executive activity, leaving the details for more comprehensive treatment in the text of the discussion. At the same time, the charts and graphs describing the outline of EOT serve as convenient reference points upon which the executive or his group may center attention.

Because of its central importance in the Executive Operations Technique, the present EOT Chart must be discussed in careful detail. An introduction to its outlines and use will be found in the following chapter.

The Practice Sessions

An intensive personal effort on the part of an individual to learn how to become an executive will, in itself, contribute substantial developmental benefits. Continued practice in identifying the purpose of an action or the usefulness of an element of material in terms of the EOT pattern establishes an intuitive familiarity with the technique. The executive is able to apply the technique without conscious reference to the EOT pattern.

But to become thoroughly familiar with tested and proved executive operating techniques, time must be provided for concentration upon this objective. Thus, at Williamson-Dickie, EOT Conferences or practice sessions have an important role.

Football teams make progress because they practice before they play. Many executives quarterback their business teams all the time but never practice. In this firm we believe it is important to set aside time for regular and frequent practice sessions.

In these conferences we rotate the chairmanship of the full group and of the smaller task committees, undertaking the study of cases drawn from the experience of the participants and from other business firms of widely divergent types. The EOT Pattern serves as the basis of discussion.

Summary   We are convinced of the value of EOT for management development and for long-range growth in our business. It is no gadget or passing fancy. It is thoroughly integrated into the whole process of management. Key elements in its integration are:

> The executives,
> The situations they face,
> The items they undertake,
> The schedules they arrange for their work,
> The EOT Chart which guides them in getting things done, and
> The practice sessions which stimulate professional performance.

II

Charting
the EOT Pattern

Several attempts have been made to represent the EOT pattern by means of graphic charts. Rectangular and circular charts have been used to show the interrelationship of the factors involved in the pattern. No chart, of course, can perfectly describe the complex mental and action processes through which an executive "gets things done through people." Schematic presentations are never as detailed as the finished product.

The present chart of the EOT pattern, however, has a number of features which will aid the serious student of management in understanding how an experienced executive deals with the situation he faces and the items he sets up for attention. While still far from being perfect, the EOT Chart is a convenient summary of EOT's main outlines and has proved to be a useful supplement in helping executives to visualize the relationships of the factors involved.

9

Emphasis Areas

Before introducing the complete EOT Chart, it may be desirable to examine the broad outlines which serve to unify the chart in a cross-classification of emphasis areas. Listed below are the Executive Considerations and Advancement Steps or areas of emphasis that are often simultaneously involved in an executive's thought and action. The six Executive Considerations and the six Advancement Steps are together known as the twelve Emphasis Areas.

THE TWELVE EMPHASIS AREAS OF EOT

Illustrating the Executive Pattern
of Thought and Action

The Executive Emphasizes These *Advancement Steps* As the Item Progresses	The Executive Should Continuously Emphasize Each of These *Considerations*
C Expose Conditions	1 Identify Subjects
I Develop Ideas	2 Express Particulars
V Unify Views	3 Analyze Relations
P Determine Plans	4 Coordinate Purposes
A Produce Actions	5 Control Certainties
R Review Results	6 Evaluate Satisfactions

The Advancement Steps in the left hand column show how an item progresses from *Expose Conditions* to *Review Results*. The six Executive Considerations on the right side of the chart guide the development of executive mastery of the situation, beginning with *Identify Subjects* and continuing through *Evaluate Satisfactions*.

The six Advancement Steps and the six Executive Considerations together suggest a sequence through which an item matures in advancement as well as depth of consideration from its start to its conclusion. All twelve areas may be taken into account by the executive at each step in the advancement of the item.

These areas are expressed in twelve verb-noun phrases under which, we believe, any executive thought or action which might advance a project can be classified. Conversely and more important, our experience has been that the twelve terms serve as stimuli to effective responses and guides to promote efficient, fruitful thinking and acting by executives on the items of work for which they are responsible. The Emphasis Areas have not been arbitrarily selected, but have evolved through years of study of executive operations.

Rational Sequence

Some may wonder why the Advancement Steps and the Executive Considerations are presented in the order shown in Figure 2. Far from being a random distribution, each set of Emphasis Areas is rationally sequenced according to typically effective executive operations.

The Advancement Steps, for example, reflect the normal sequence an item moves through in its progress toward completion. In the same way the executive's thought processes, in contemplating the future course of the item, move through these logical steps. Thus, the successful executive will expose conditions underlying the situation he faces, develop ideas concerning possible solutions, unify the views of those who will be most intimately concerned with the problem, determine plans, produce actions which will complete the item, and finally review the results obtained. This rational sequence reflects currently accepted practices in executive decision-making as well as in logical philosophy.

The Executive Considerations are also sequenced according to rational design, reflecting the levels of depth at which an executive considers the item and its progress. First, he will seek to identify the subject under scrutiny. Second, the particulars of the situation from which the item has been developed will be expressed. Third, he will analyze the relations involved. Fourth will be the coordination of the purposes among the many people and things usually enmeshed with the progress of an item. Fifth, the executive will attempt to control the item to assure certainty in the matching of intentions and results. Finally, he will evaluate his satisfactions with the item's progress.

Interrelated Areas

The interrelated nature of these areas is illustrated by the executive's use of each Executive Consideration at each Advancement Step. The executive, for example, Exposes Conditions by Identifying Subjects, Develops Ideas by Expressing Particulars, and Unifies Views by Analyzing Relations. In each of these examples, one may note, the Step is related to the Consideration.

Likewise the Consideration is reciprocally related to the Step. Thus, an executive Identifies Subjects when Exposing Conditions, Analyzes

Relations when Developing Ideas, and Coordinates Purposes when Unifying Views.

Emphasis Areas Provoke Questions

The concept of an Executive Operating Technique had its origin in an attempt to classify and categorize questions that executives ask. The first major category was the advancement cycle through which an item progresses. It was perceived as early as 1942 that executives ask different types of questions relating to conditions, ideas, plans, views, actions, and results. The concept of the Advancement Steps, when firmly planted in the mind of an executive, enables him to project the future course of an item. He will ask discerning questions not only of others but of himself as well.

If the executive's concept of the advancement cycle is clear and unequivocal, searching questions will "naturally" occur to him as he looks ahead at the steps to come and as he looks back on steps just past.

The other major category of questions envelops the Executive Considerations. Here the competent executive will ask (of himself and others, again) such questions as:

"What *subjects* are involved?"
"How are these elements *related?*"
"How can the particulars be *expressed?*'
"What *purposes* must be served?"
"How *certain* are you (am I)?"
"Are you (Am I) *satisfied?*"

Each of the consideration areas then provokes particular kinds of searching questions.

Steps and Considerations Distinguished

An explanation may be needed at this point to distinguish between Advancement Steps and Executive Considerations. The Advancement Steps represent end-products of the executive operations efforts and techniques. The Advancement Steps or their end-product—for example, a developed idea or determined plan—could only come through adequate use of the considerations by the executive. Possession of the end-products exemplified by each advancement step will, in itself, permit the executive to consider the situation or item in greater depth. It also permits a new application of the consideration, such as identifying subjects, analyzing relations, and so forth.

The performance of each of the Advancement Steps brings new material into consideration. Consideration of this material by an executive with adequate capacity to identify subjects, express particulars, analyze relations, coordinate purposes, control certainties, and evaluate satisfactions causes the item to advance in maturity of consideration. Getting the item through each advancement step provides objective material for further executive consideration.

The executive should improve his capacity for executive consideration in each of the six emphasis areas represented.

The Advancement Steps may be looked upon by the executive as goals to achieve, goals which when achieved permit consideration in greater maturity. The reciprocal or alternating application of both thought and action by the executive carries the item through to a successful and productive conclusion.

Guide Points in Emphasis Areas

For quite some time, the EOT framework consisted principally of the emphasis areas outlined in the previous paragraphs. As these were refined and used operationally, it became clear that an additional category of useful techniques could be distinguished within the broader outlines of the Advancement Steps and the Executive Considerations. Definition of these more concrete techniques within the framework of the emphasis areas resulted in a group of 144 "imperative sentences" which became known as *guide points*.

A schematic view of several of these guide points may be seen in Figure 2. This chart introduces one guide point into each of several cells where the steps and the considerations intersect. Each of the guide points, it will be noted, are examples of ways in which the executive can utilize a specific technique to encourage the progress of an item. Reference to each guide point will provide the executive with clues to more effective operations.

Originally, these guide points evolved from an inductive study of what specific thoughts and actions can be discovered in executive operations as the successive advancement steps are planned, performed, and reviewed. This study resulted in a lengthy list of techniques or tools in the competent executive's kit. There was no particular attempt to be encyclopedic as only the commonly used and typically effective techniques were sorted from among the great number of suggested guide points.

A parallel study of techniques emphasized in the course of the executive considerations brought forth another list of guide points projected along the horizontal dimension of the chart. This list was also reduced to the most effective number.

These two attempts at specifying the more abstract concepts found in the Emphasis Areas appeared to heighten interest and comprehension. Participating executives found that they could classify their daily activities by both Emphasis Area and Guide Point. Further along, a study of the relationships among the two lists revealed considerable overlapping. That is, many of the guide points were found to be effective in the advancement cycle and among the executive considerations.

Realization of this cross-relationship led in 1953 to drafting the complete EOT Chart shown in Figure 3. This chart is a symmetrical arrangement of the guide points as they can best be classified within the steps in the advancement cycle and the levels of executive consideration.

Even a cursory examination of the guide points listed on the chart will reveal that some are more obvious and some are more subtle than others. Varying degrees of sophistication and abstraction can be seen in all. Therefore, each of the guide points is discussed in some detail in later chapters.

For the time being, however, it is sufficient to state that these 144 guide points should serve as reminders or prompters to an executive as he moves through his management activity. They will often provide insight into problems facing the organization or the executive group. The terminology, while perhaps new and unusual, will be a distinct aid in communicating information among the management group. This is particularly true once the guide points are mastered through study of the exposition and case illustrations dealing with each guide point.

Our practice up to this time in developing an EOT indicates, as in the systems of music and chemistry, it is a "closed system." As a working hypothesis, however, this closed system need not be perfect to serve as a means of common communication within the executive group. Any instance of "content element" appearing in any executive situation will be provided for within the Chart of Executive Operations Techniques. The system is closed around the full scope of executive operations, and any executive act or responding consideration may be positioned somewhere on the chart. If the system does not provide for this "content element" within its framework, then (under our present thought) we

EOT CHART

ADVANCEMENT STEPS

EXECUTIVE CONSIDERATIONS

	EXPOSE CONDITIONS	DEVELOP IDEAS	UNIFY VIEWS	DETERMINE PLANS	PRODUCE ACTIONS	REVIEW RESULTS
1. IDENTIFY SUBJECTS	Expose conditions by identifying subjects; e.g., through Collecting Sources					
2. EXPRESS PARTICULARS		Develop ideas by expressing particulars; e.g., through Suggesting Recommendations				
3. ANALYZE RELATIONS			Unify views by analyzing relations; e.g., through Mediating Group Opinions			
4. COORDINATE PURPOSES				Determine plans by coordinating purposes; e.g., through Foreseeing Strategies		
5. CONTROL CERTAINTIES					Produce actions by controlling certainties; e.g., through Emphasizing Advancements	
6. EVALUATE SATISFACTIONS						Review results by evaluating satisfactions; e.g., through Weighing Improvements

FIGURE 2. SCHEMATIC RELATION OF STEPS, CONSIDERATIONS, AND GUIDE POINTS.

EOT CHART

ADVANCEMENT STEPS

EXECUTIVE CONSIDERATIONS

	EXPOSE CONDITIONS	DEVELOP IDEAS	UNIFY VIEWS	DETERMINE PLANS	PRODUCE ACTIONS	REVIEW RESULTS
1. IDENTIFY SUBJECTS	1 Collect Sources 2 Observe Evidence 3 Receive Statements 4 Question Implications	1 Fill Out Full Scope 2 Evolve Alternatives 3 Differentiate Distinctions 4 Visualize Concepts	1 Recognize Individuals 2 Share Interests 3 Encourage Flexibilities 4 Clarify Misunderstandings	1 Comprehend Policies 2 Define Objectives 3 Undertake Items 4 Create Next Steps	1 Conduct Pilot Experiments 2 Interpret Assignments 3 Study Approaches 4 Initiate Participations	1 Hold Conferences 2 Inspect Changes 3 Recall Notations 4 Assemble Records
2. EXPRESS PARTICULARS	1 Describe Understandings 2 List Contents 3 Figure Costs 4 Supply Exhibits	1 Suggest Recommendations 2 Calculate Ratios 3 Multiply Applications 4 Formulate Measurements	1 Submit Propositions 2 Reveal Positions 3 Introduce Data 4 Offer Reasons	1 Write Details 2 Designate Titles 3 Estimate Expectations 4 Design Forms	1 Explain Intentions 2 Follow Reminders 3 Apply Formulas 4 Complete Answers	1 Ascertain Actuals 2 Record Activities 3 Count Inventories 4 Total Units
3. ANALYZE RELATIONS	1 Discover Involvements 2 Relate Factors 3 Project Dimensions 4 Circumscribe Inclusions	1 Associate Similarities 2 Infer Breakdown Schemes 3 Isolate Separables 4 Cross-Fertilize Contributions	1 Balance Dominances 2 Communicate Information 3 Combine Inclinations 4 Mediate Group Opinions	1 Integrate Compatible Factors 2 Lay Out Cross-Classifications 3 Organize Functions 4 Assign Accountabilities	1 Utilize Availables 2 Adapt to Developments 3 Overcome Obstacles 4 Consult Advisers	1 Align Comparables 2 Compare Entries 3 Break Down Deviations 4 Compute Indexes
4. COORDINATE PURPOSES	1 Investigate Backgrounds 2 Start Preliminaries 3 Arrange Facilities 4 Date Progressions	1 Perceive Time Openings 2 Pace Assimilations 3 Incubate Refinements 4 Classify Usefuls	1 Continue Contacts 2 Tie in Transitions 3 Accept Responsibilities 4 Build Permanencies	1 Sequence Efforts 2 Synchronize Schedules 3 Proceduralize Routines 4 Foresee Strategies	1 Reconsider Requirements 2 Move Back Emphasis Area 3 Activate Idlers 4 Meet Deadlines	1 Revise Obsoletes 2 Check Previous Periods 3 Detect Trends 4 Index References
5. CONTROL CERTAINTIES	1 Disclose Sufficiencies 2 Criticize Controllables 3 Exhaust Possibilities 4 Establish Controls	1 Assume Tentatives 2 Support Insights 3 Provide Risk Margins 4 Verify Accuracies	1 Condition Atmosphere 2 Reconcile Inconsistencies 3 Stratify Confidences 4 Agree on Courses	1 Declare Standards 2 Eliminate Non-essentials 3 Anticipate Contingencies 4 Qualify Commitments	1 Intensify Determinations 2 Emphasize Advancements 3 Account for Modifications 4 Test Completions	1 Preserve Experiences 2 Carry Over Knowns 3 Survey Consequences 4 Acknowledge Realities
6. EVALUATE SATISFACTIONS	1 Sense Defects 2 Select Opportunities 3 Summarize Situations 4 Attack Key Issues	1 Simplify by Reduction 2 Shift Scopes 3 Modify Reservations 4 Face Present Needs	1 Appraise Tolerations 2 Respond to Probable Effects 3 Rely on Convictions 4 Desire Advantages	1 Find Criteria 2 Rank Selections 3 Authorize Decisions 4 Release Agreements	1 Handle Non-completions 2 Moderate Refinement Extremes 3 Reprocess Inadequacies 4 Report Accomplishments	1 Weigh Improvements 2 Reevaluate Techniques 3 Suspend Influences 4 Feed Back Cycles

EOT Chart Copyright 1961

FIGURE 3.

must either improve or learn to orient ourselves to the most logical positioning of the point.

At first glance this closed system may cause an executive to feel discomfort. His orientation to the terms at the beginning may not readily accommodate his customary usage or interpretations. On the other hand, maintaining a central, logical structure is akin in its favorable effect to standardization and simplification. The adjustment to the structure will return long-run benefits which will enrich and give a deeper meaning to the knowledge of the executive.

SUMMARY   The EOT Chart represents a culmination of years of effort to refine and distill the essential elements in successful executive operations. The broad outlines of the pattern can be sketched in a variety of ways, using circular flow charts and tabular cross-classifications. The graphic technique illustrates the fundamental importance of the Emphasis Areas, which consist of six Advancement Steps and six Executive Considerations. Each step in the advancement cycle and each consideration is sequenced in rational order; each is interrelated with all the others. A noteworthy feature of the Emphasis Areas is their property of provoking discerning questions concerning the item's progress.

Guide points are more specific indicators of typically effective executive techniques. They often serve as reminders that executives should investigate particular logical approaches to the solution of problems facing them. To be operationally useful, the guide points must be mastered in terms of both their theory and application. In the discussion beginning Chapter IV, the EOT guide points have been arbitrarily separated to develop a greater familiarity with each individual guide point than would be possible if they were seen collectively. One should not approach a situation, however, with a preconceived assumption that any one guide point is more likely to be found than another unless he has some preliminary information to suggest this assumption. Before turning to discussion of the guide points which will indirectly bear on the advancement sequence, more attention will be given to the general concept of advancement steps in Chapter III.

III

Advancement Steps

A familiar concept to persons dealing with the decision-making process is that problem solving occurs in recognizable steps. These steps may be identified in many ways, using a wide variety of terms. Nevertheless, there is a remarkable fundamental agreement among those who have studied and described the logical process by which decisions are reached in business organizations.

Because these ultimate decisions result from executives devoting persistent effort and skill to particular problems, it is also possible to trace the sequence of steps through which an item passes as it moves from beginning to end. One participating executive may contribute primarily to only a limited number of steps, while others may concentrate upon the other steps as an item advances. But, in both contemplation and retrospect, the item itself advances through identifiable steps. The supervising executive must not allow the item to bog down within any step nor permit it to be moved through an advancement step before adequate considerations have been brought to bear.

The sequence of steps by which an item is advanced has been described earlier in brief. The six Advancement Steps are: *Expose Conditions, Develop Ideas, Unify Views, Determine Plans, Produce Action,* and *Review Results.* In this chapter, each of the steps is considered in order and in greater depth.

Exposing Conditions

Repeated experimentation with executive operations on undertaken items has led to the conclusion that the first step in the advancement of an item is the Exposing of Conditions. For centuries, men have recognized that logical decisions cannot be reached without prior careful study of the conditions underlying any situation. Investigators in science and industry must first uncover and study the prevailing fact conditions. Only then may they move ahead into the development of ideas for solving the problems thus identified.

The conditions that the executive seeks to expose in this step are those factors existing within a situation which will influence or determine the nature of his operations. These conditions are viewed in the context of looking forward in the advancement cycle, but the same facts can be viewed retrospectively as results within the previous cycle's context.

When a cycle of action has been completed, when no future action is contemplated, and when a mere *post mortem* is the purpose, the terminal findings may then be results. In this way, the nature of operating information and its usefulness is dependent to a large degree upon the advancement along the action cycle.

There may be a stock or inventory of conditions accumulated over a period of time that influences prospective success or failure. The working capital of a business, the number of customers, and their good will are examples of such conditions. These same facts, however, if viewed in a context in which they follow a cycle of action, become results. It is the precedence in the cycle—this forward look into time—that transforms the same facts from results to conditions.

Executives working with conditions usually intend to use them to influence a situation favorably in the future. The conditions produced in the past cannot be changed, of course, except in the future.

Of great importance to the advancement of an item is concentration upon this one step of Exposing Conditions until its possibilities have been exhausted. Attractive ideas should be noted but tabled for later use after the relevant conditions have been adequately exposed. Then the development of those ideas and others may be emphasized.

Developing Ideas

Ideas are visualizations of more advanced conditions than those currently existing in a situation. Ideas take on a freshness or potency to the executive when they apply to conditions existing within a particular situation with which he is concerned. Ideas irrelevant to some felt or expressed need probably should not qualify as ideas at all. If the executive is dealing with a specific problem, then the visualization of a possible action that suggests a performable solution is an idea. Views take their direction from and plans are based upon ideas developed in this step.

To develop means to alter operating material favorably. The activity of developing causes a subject or situation to evolve from a potential or latent condition to a more usable form. This change implies an improvement.

A creative, progressive attitude is necessary to the most productive development of ideas from operating material. An executive developing a helpful idea usually helps the company while he enjoys the experience and gains prestige among his associates. Each member of a cooperating group should be able to answer favorably the question, "What have I contributed?" The spirit of the group should be to respond constructively and not defensively, and each individual should strive for advancement and assist others in developing solutions. Negative, irrelevant, or indefinite cooperation in developing ideas must be compensated by extra effort by others in the group. This is somewhat analogous to the situation where several products are in the manufacturer's line. If a gross profit of 25 per cent must be maintained and one product falls to 22 per cent, some other product of equal volume must yield 28 per cent in order to maintain the average and offset the relative loss.

Realizing the distinction between fixed and controllable conditions is fundamental to producing workable ideas. There should also be a unified, undistracted emphasis upon idea development at this step. An executive is probably in better mental condition to develop ideas when he has completed all the routine business on his schedule. But, on the other hand, the adage "Necessity is the mother of invention" has often proved true.

The encouragement of ideas in a management group may be a type of husbandry. The conditions are prepared for the propagation of ideas in the selected area of activity. When ideas are developed, emphasis is upon this one step and not upon conditions, views, action, or any other emphasis area. The climate, light, atmosphere, and soil in which ideas are planted are just as important for the propagation of ideas as they are for maturing of a seed. When first sprouted, ideas need proper care and feeding. If they are selected from a hardy strain—grounded in facts —they are more likely to survive the buffeting of the natural elements, pests, and other hazards. An atmosphere conducive to developing ideas might be described as one in which all members of the organization are encouraged to share in this creative satisfaction.

The purpose of developing ideas is to fill out a necessary link in the advancement cycle. It sets up material that may be used in a plan. In addition to the material benefits to which ideas lead, there are great personal satisfactions in creative development.

Ideas are the material around which the views of individuals concerned must be unified before the item may advance further. If well developed and carefully selected, workable ideas can be processed swiftly through the next step in the item's advancement. Ideas may apply to one-time use in a situation or to improving a method or approach which may be used repeatedly in similar situations.

Unifying Views

After accumulated ideas have been developed into a rudimentary pattern, they are usually exposed to the views of others. This exposure brings out the personal preferences, attitudes, values, and beliefs of people who are important to further advance the item. If their views are favorable to the item's progress, the executive will not have the problem of unifying divergent views.

The purpose of this step in the advancement cycle is to unite the individual positions toward a common objective. Assuming that ideas previously developed are valid and worthy of support, the end desired is to enlist the cooperation of the other individuals so they support the full scope of the understanding.

The choice between advancing the item and dwelling upon a prevailing but retarding view presents a frequent opportunity for unifying views. The individual whose views are under consideration is affected by his own subjective reactions and by external influences. Orienting to this external factor is significant in dealing with views. A self-centered individual is more likely to have non-constructive views than a situation-centered person. Depersonalizing operating material is frequently accomplished by identifying the material before it is evaluated. A statement of the fundamental conditions confronting all members of the group usually has greater influence than lesser individual differences; petty objections will often disappear.

The chairman or leader may frequently emphasize description rather than evaluation during early stages of a conference. He may, if conditions should suggest, use indirect approaches to a proposition. Such a discussion may bring out strong and weak points of the situation, with no adverse reflection on any individual.

Once the views of the executives and other individuals concerned have been sufficiently unified, the supervising executive will be ready to prepare the detailed plans for action.

Determining Plans

Plans are arrangements of intended occurrences determined in advance to serve as guides to the production of results. They guide intended actions as well as areas of consideration to be emphasized. Plans are, therefore, a major ingredient of successful executive operations.

Plans are determined for a specific purpose, usually in connection with a particular situation. Obviously, they should be determined in advance of objective action, but many executives wait until just before action is required to make a decision. The habit of deciding well in advance has to be cultivated by the executive.

Edwin G. Booz always emphasized the importance of planning in advance whenever possible. Consulting with us, he often stressed the need to plan more. Constantly looking ahead and determining in advance was something we had not gone out of the way to do. Instead, we planned in advance only the issues absolutely required in our operations. Some difficult or distasteful decisions were left until just before their deadlines. Sales estimates for the purpose of planning inventories, material purchases, and production schedules were reluctantly made. Many other personal plans, such as necessary business trips, were not determined in advance.

Decisions made in advance and with foresight should be looked upon as no more difficult than any other decisions. All executives should look forward with some satisfaction to getting decisions behind them. Such advance planning promotes a greater feeling of security and serenity among an operating group.

Plans facilitate group operation upon an objective. If a sizable group is working without plans, confusion will result. Sound plans, on which the group is unified and coordinated, help to concentrate efforts upon primary goals.

A practice or customary method is not necessarily termed a plan in the EOT cycle although it may appear as a described action or job. Some types of plans, as we use the term, may require no influence on results from the planning executive. Estimates or forecasts of general business are this type.

A military operations order is a plan, as is a specific assignment. Recommendations or matters awaiting approval are plan components, at least at the level of the individual making the recommendation. In fact, a decision is quite a pointed plan—as are concluded alternatives, content elements, and ideas, once they reach the maturity of advancement awaiting determination at a higher executive level.

Some plans such as standards are useful repeatedly and automatically. Procedures are plans which may be used repeatedly to guide action from start to finish. An organization chart may be continuously useful in channeling functions and relations. Departmentation, as represented in organization charts, guides the application of actions, skills, and communication.

The act of determining involves reaching a mental conclusion, usually regarding a choice of ideas or possible alternatives. Normally, determination includes the consideration of relevant factors exposed through reasoning and investigation before reaching a conclusion.

The precedence of unification of views before the determination of plans in the advancement cycle has already been stressed. This has a practical bearing on authority—not only on the authority vested in a managerial position, but on the authority inherent in a valid plan. Such a plan should be in alignment with the needs of the situation as well as with the broad strategy of the company.

The conditions permitting the plan to represent prospective action with certainty are suggested in the first three Advancement Steps. Adequate ideas, for example, are necessary factors to facilitate effective determination. At the time plans are determined, the executive gets his last look at the item before it goes into action, assuming, of course, that the plans are determined in advance of action. One of the major characteristics of plans is their prospective nature. Action and results may never be produced according to the exact pattern of the plans. Nevertheless, plans are one of the underlying agencies through which management operates.

Unless planning is cultivated so that it can be done with some relish, it may become a distasteful chore. According to a statement made by J. O. McKinsey, "Planning is the tangible evidence of the thinking of management." Under any circumstances, the determined plan is the agency through which management harnesses the cooperative skills and energies of the management group.

Producing Actions

There comes a time in the advancement cycle in which the emphasis is on objective action and no longer upon preparatory steps. When this point in the cycle is reached, the executive must start actions which produce tangible results. The main emphasis is upon producing actions— not upon determining plans or any of the preceding steps.

Action is the operation of forces upon a situation for the purpose of advancement toward satisfactory results. Action is an occurrence which causes change in a situation. Executive operations seek to influence this change so that its outcome is favorable.

Action is not an illusion. To the pedestrian, the danger of an onrushing car may be said by some to be an illusion, because it has not yet hit him. Theoretically, we may need to consummate the three requirements of reality: time, space, and the event. The momentum of the car at the time the pedestrian sees it approaching, however, is a tangible reality which has a measurable physical force. By the same reasoning, executive action builds up its own momentum within the participating individuals. Potential energy or latent executive action exists in the drive and tenacity of the executives in an organization.

Action may be described as the process of reaching a given terminal point. When this completion is produced, the action has terminated. Any given event, advancement, or transaction represents particular measurable or countable entities of action which may be completed.

Of course, actions of a sort have been produced in exposing conditions and developing ideas. The unification of views also has been the focal scope of productive effort along the way. The motivation of those who are to contribute is imperative in getting full approval for the course of action. This motivation requires a certain kind of action.

Necessity is a powerful motive to action, and such actions have a definite purpose. Some actions, on the other hand, are accidental. Actions may be necessary and achieve the results desired, or unnecessary and do nothing to advance the item. Improvised or unplanned actions generally fail to advance the item as effectively as previously planned actions.

The opposites to action are frequently referred to as inaction, neglect, and "talk without doing." Sometimes, too, inertia or the "novelty wearing off" prohibits action.

If effective actions are not producible because of defects or deficiencies in previous steps, the executive may be forced to move back his emphasis area and start over again. Thus begins a new cycle, the results of the original cycle being considered inadequate.

Sometimes executives are faced with situations with very few clues for a suitable starting place. In such cases, results may be produced through action only by application of effort or drive. Often after intensive effort is sustained, experience will reveal productive areas. This statement is based upon the assumption that the action is purposeful, as capricious action is an abuse of purposeful action. It is also well to remember that the personal activity of the executive is not necessarily a measure of item advancement. The item advances by the effective and action-producing operation of the whole executive group.

Consistent action-awareness along with time-awareness is needed to bring about results for review in the next step.

Reviewing Results

Reviewing results, the last step in the item advancement cycle, is one of the most frequently emphasized in the cycle of exe utive activity. It marks a vital point in the advancement cycle. Favorable consequences are usually the executive's aim, but frequently action and particularly inconclusive action do not always produce satisfactory results. There is at this point a finality to results until a new cycle of advancement is entered upon and completed.

Many of the advancements in executive operations are in definiteness and depth of knowledge of a particular undertaking. Examples are: identifying a subject, formulating an expression, and analyzing relations.

Results may be conceived in terms of production activity in number of units. This familiar aspect emphasizes the results attained within a period of time. Another way of looking at results, however, is to view them as stock or inventory at a given time—possibly, as a collection or an accumulation.

If an executive is skillful in dealing with figures, the expression of results may be handled definitely and without undue effort. The scope limits of the item should outline the full scope of results. The time period and the total units in figures may further specify results.

Results can be qualitative as well as quantitative. For effective action and consideration, it is usually better to concentrate on producing only one type of results at any particular time. A manufacturing problem is simpler if either an increase in production or an improvement in quality is sought but not both in any one undertaken item.

Emphasis should be kept upon results rather than on conditions. Since completion is generally more interesting and productive than incompletion, this final step is also a convenient point for key executives personally to review the situation.

The natural urge to ask "Why?" should be suspended or restrained at this step. Questioning results frequently leads to exposing causes of success or failure. As a result, effort is set in motion prematurely for the cycle to follow. Attention is diverted from a retrospective view of the cycle just completed. For this reason, one should continue emphasis upon reviewing the cycle of advancement under study, in order to exhaust retrospective knowledge of the item's progress.

To be operationally valid, favorable results should have been planned previously. Otherwise, they might be considered merely good luck.

SUMMARY   The six Advancement Steps describe a process or cycle that each unit of executive work moves through on its way toward completion. Each step must be emphasized in its appropriate location in the item's time-span; premature or tardy emphasis will impede or obstruct the item. Executives would do well to concentrate upon each step in turn. The rational sequence through which an item advances is that of exposing conditions, developing ideas, unifying views, determining plans, producing action, and reviewing results.

Advancement of an item, however, requires consideration in depth at each step. The guide points from experience, therefore, have been consolidated for discussion under the six consideration areas in the following chapters. Each chapter in turn is arranged in the sequence of the advancement steps.

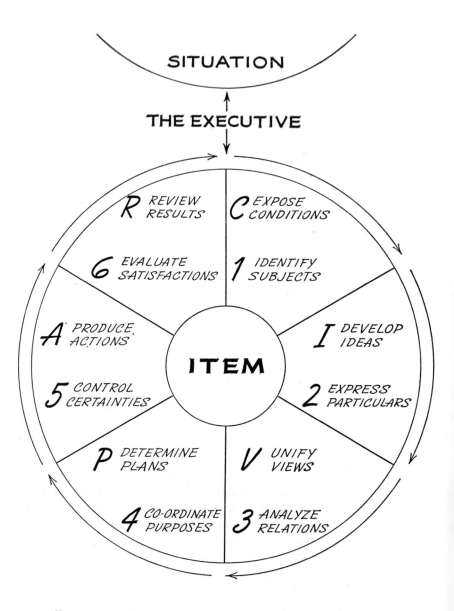

FIGURE 4. THE SITUATION, THE EXECUTIVE, AND THE ITEM.

IV

Identifying Subjects

Subjects, their consideration, and the actions produced within their limits have profound effects upon an enterprise and upon the people connected with it. Executives deal almost constantly with subjects.

A subject is the visualized representation of an object of discussion or attention and is the central frame of reference in the activity or consideration. It may range in detail from a name or number (in its thinnest telegraphic sense) through fuller descriptive exposition to the full context of a manuscript. In relative time maturity, a subject may range from a preliminary hypothesis before experience to a conclusion after long observation.

A subject is a unit of executive consideration that is susceptible to manipulation. Thus, an executive may introduce a subject during a conference. He may dwell on the subject, exhaust it, change it, abandon it, or come back to it. On the other hand, he may plan to discuss it, even though he may never reach it.

Identifying is an activity that produces an understanding of a subject in the mind of an individual. Therefore, almost anything done to clarify, to remove indefiniteness, or to make a subject or situation more clear and unmistakable in meaning would be identifying. Identifying is the visualizing of a subject for what it is rather than simply for what it is not.

Identifying a subject requires that the executive intellectually master the subject to a depth of insight and understanding adequate to the purpose. This involves an optimal objective and may include the full scope, its parts and their relations, and other similar considerations. Segmentation of the content or substance of a subject into its particulars and their subsequent recall should help identify a subject.

Identification starts with outlining a manageable segment of operating material. After these subjects are made definite, they are transmissible as units of communication or thought. These elements of content may represent any unit of executive material, such as a part of a situation or any object of consideration. Executives are thus required to reduce subjects to a definiteness convenient to handle. Some types of subjects lend themselves to this form of visualization better than others. Economic information about merchandise and its activity may be easier to visualize definitely than social information about the behavior of people. Technical information about methods may be somewhere between.

Identifying is an activity shared in common with others. If consideration is pointed toward a situation, frequently others are found concentrating upon the same situation. If communicants referring to the same entity select the same or closely synonymous terms to express understanding of it, mutual identification will probably result. Discussion will usually proceed until an exception occurs in the form of a "misunderstanding" or defect in identity, and then more emphasis upon the identifying activity is needed.

Identifying with words depends on how well the involved individuals are equipped to understand. Executives need to understand the meaning of words in order both to express and receive communications. Everyone acquires a general vocabulary of his native language. After years of careful thought concerning subtle technical problems of garment manufacturing, a special terminology has become useful in that particular field of activity. Executives also have a language pattern in which terms may have precise and limited meanings. These terms are not many, but they should be used only with full understanding of their customary meaning.

Correct prononunication does not necessarily indicate knowledge of a word's meaning. But when an individual mispronounces a word, it can often be concluded that he does not know its meaning. If he knows how to pronounce the word correctly but still misuses it, others will have to resort to more indirect means of identifying the subjects he is talking about.

The four elements involved in identification are: (1) the referred-to entity, (2) the individuals involved, (3) their central visualized identification of this entity, and (4) their vocabulary patterns.

Some authorities call identifying from direct experience extensional orientation. This is the realistic identifying used frequently in executive operations. Intensional orientation is the term sometimes given the second type of identification—identifying with words. Neither means of identification should be used to the exclusion of the other. Used in balance, both strengthen and supplement each other.

The guide points found useful especially in Identifying Subjects are discussed now under each of the Advancement Steps.

IDENTIFYING SUBJECTS: EXPOSE CONDITIONS

C 1–1: *Collect Sources*

An early step in the exposure of conditions is the seeking and finding of sources of information. These sources are the places, individuals, and facilities from which operating material is drawn.

Records are always good sources of information, but it is frequently helpful to turn to other sources near at hand. For example, if a production line operation is causing trouble, the operation as it is then being performed should be studied. Such a simple, informal start may avoid duplicated effort. Often the nearest person to the situation, such as a machine operator, is a good source of information. With such persons, it is highly desirable to cultivate a willingness to supply information.

When time is available, books and professional journals suggest areas to explore. Such literature usually shows the present thinking in the field with clues to typical schemes of organization or analysis used in dealing with the subject.

Collecting sources of information is one of the principal specialities of many professions such as law and engineering. Consultants often contribute by introducing techniques for a deeper exposure of conditions.

Up to a few years ago, the conditions of success or failure of William-son-Dickie's product designs were exposed by talking to a few dealers and our own Sales Department personnel. Opinion research led us to expose conditions in an orderly and exhaustive way through other sources, such as consumers (many of them employees), dealers, and salesmen. If only those with organizational status and prestige, are queried, some primary sources of information are likely to be overlooked.

In collecting sources, certain conditions influence the success or failure of the activity. Curiosity is one of these conditions. An individual's eager desire to learn frequently makes this step a pleasant and rewarding activity.

C 1–2: Observe Evidence

Written reports or exhibits may supplement an oral discussion. Examination of written evidence may be more productive in exposing conditions than oral reports alone. When the observation area is reduced to a scope sufficiently narrow for experience, exposure of information is frequently more effective.

The recognition of evidence as being condition factors that influence the success or failure of an undertaking is in itself a form of subject identification. The executive who has observed the evidence at first hand or through direct experience is more likely to understand the situation. Information passed through several people can create opportunities for misunderstanding.

Failure to read promptly references or reports relating to a subject under consideration constitutes neglect of the Observe Evidence guide point.

C 1–3: Receive Statements

Many times others offer to the executive information in the form of statements. In receiving these statements, the executive listens for the purpose of gathering information. Much information is not immediately obvious, and unless he listens attentively and observes good listening habits, he may fail to learn of conditions critical to the success of his undertaking. He must, as a Williamson-Dickie vice-president has said, "stay on the 'phone."

A good listener usually asks for more information on points inadequately identified, and does not pass over material which is difficult to comprehend. Listening opportunities should not be sacrificed to the temptation to make rebuttals or to decide before hearing the full story.

Sometimes upon being asked questions to expose conditions, the person being interviewed creates obstacles because he does not answer the question asked. His answer may be incomplete, thus requiring the listener to complete the statement or, in the case of a question for figures, to carry calculations further by averaging or totaling. Others make a complex or wordy answer with little substance instead of simply saying, "I don't know" or "I will find out." The competent executive can often indicate his dissatisfaction with such replies without cutting off future communication opportunities.

Since this is still an early stage of exposing conditions, the executive should be selective yet flexible in dealing with the material. He should avoid evaluation and arrangement of facts too early. In a somewhat random fashion, he must "move the furniture into the room" before he "straightens it out."

The executive also must find out whether he is receiving the sense of the statement as the speaker intended it. Further questioning will sometimes reveal that the scope visualized by the speaker will be significantly different from that assumed by the listener. A statement may be considered to be an amplification of a subject's meaning and can, accordingly, create further understanding or misunderstanding.

C 1–4: Question Implications

Asking questions is one of the most frequently used techniques for gaining information. In fact, the EOT Emphasis Areas were first suggested by categories of typical questions. That questions are elemental and natural is shown by our intimate familiarity with the basic interrogative words: what, why, when, how, where, and who. These one-syllable words came naturally into language very early in human history.

Sometimes facts or conditions are assumed or implied without question or discussion. Questions asked to test whether information is intended to be included in or excluded from a subject will help executives to align their identification. Questions are often asked both by those who are expected to contribute information as well as by those who are seeking information.

Questions are frequently used to clarify implications. These implications are clues to meanings suggested in a statement over and beyond that of the literal wording alone. Context, intention, or tone of the speaker may provoke some implications. Likewise, the listener's background with respect to the material presented may provoke other implications.

Some understandings left in the realm of the implication may become intuitively established terms or symbols. An erroneous "understanding" is easily established especially when no effort is made to learn the meaning or the sense in which the term is being used.

Example:

The General Manager was describing a suggested approach to studying a problem manufacturing operation to an engineer. A mechanic was listening. The General Manager continued, "Check anything that might contribute to low efficiency speed of the machine, condition of the work upon its arrival at the operation, and particularly the work holding fixtures from which the operator picks up." The mechanic said, "That is right, *fixed conditions,*" which has an entirely different meaning in EOT than he had implied. Fixed conditions would not have been controllable by the engineer as were those suggested by the General Manager.

Skill in asking questions and in getting answers varies greatly among executives. A skillful questioner usually is an able fact-finder. His careful examination into the considerations underlying his questions will yield better questions and more complete responses.

Questions of the following type are frequently used by executives:

"What do you mean by that?"
"What are you insulating it with?"
"Where are you measuring?"

Some questions, of course, generate substance, while others are definitive.

Questions are used more formally in surveys, guided interviews, and questionnaires. Opinion research is used effectively in exposing conditions that influence the success or failure of product acceptance by consumers.

IDENTIFYING SUBJECTS: DEVELOP IDEAS

I 1–1: Fill Out Full Scope

Executives must be capable of seeing the full scope of a problem situation facing them. To do this, they must often gather together incomplete fragments of data and information so that all the ramifications of the problem can be considered adequately. In doing this, they must frequently guard against overemphasizing some segments of a situation at the expense of the full scope.

Previous experience or a sense of logical order may be the stimulating motive for filling out the full scope of a pattern. If a four-fingered hand is sketched with the thumb missing, an individual tends to fill out the pattern with the thumb, making a simple, complete, five-element pattern. When several elements of a scheme form an incomplete pattern, he looks for the completing element. Given north, south, and east, he can apply west as the fourth and completing element in a four-part geographical scheme. If he aggregates these parts into a pattern, he has filled out the full scope to a point that is complete within itself.

The ability to fill out the full scope is essential to executives on all management levels. Each functional executive must consider how his decisions will affect the coordination of purposes within the entire organization. The sales manager, for example, must be able to foresee the effects of a new decision, policy, or program not only upon the company sales but on production as well. He must consider its effects on the company as a whole as well as its parts. In a limited fashion, each executive has a responsibility similar to that of the president or the general manager—to fill out the full scope of all items affecting the several areas of his direct responsibility.

A business example of filling out the full scope of a situation might take place when the Product Research Director is looking for sources of information on the merits of his company's products. He has a partially complete pattern, including the categories of "consumers," "dealers," and "salesmen." The scope might be filled out or completed by adding "competitors." The required category to fill out the scope may also be suggested by the presence of material which will not fit any of the other categories already in the breakdown scheme.

I 1–2: Evolve Alternatives

Opportunities exist after a condition is identified, and it is seen that something should be done about it. Possible solutions or alternatives arising at this point are ideas. Research aims ultimately at developing ideas, although most of its efforts may center upon exposing conditions by analyzing relations, controlling certainty, and other activities. Exposed conditions are sources of ideas. The ideas themselves are frequently not self-evident but must result from creative thinking through insights gained from successful experience.

In evolving alternatives, the executive intensifies his efforts as he searches for a possible course of action from those available. He looks for solutions and favorable alternatives emphasizing the creation of ideas at this point. One common error is to evolve only one alternative, expecting it alone to be sufficient. If this alternative is later found to be inadequate or insufficient, the executive may then be at a loss. On the other hand, good executive practice provides an overabundance of alternatives for consideration and action at this step.

Like many other manufacturers, we have searched aggressively for opportunities to increase each of our dealers' sales so that the aggregate increase in dealer sales would result in increased sales for our company. One such idea developed into the Dickie Dealer Profit Plan. In this our salesmen have the advantage of selling the dealer "sales" and "profits" in addition to tangible products. Evolving the numerous alternatives proffered which would fulfill our principal objectives culminated in an effective sales promotion device. A number of the evolved alternatives were discarded or stored away but the best were utilized in the plan.

Some solutions are inadequate because they are too indefinite or general. More likely, however, they do not provide for sufficiently potent alternatives. The solution may contain only the obvious alternatives which take little effort. Sometimes the alternative provides only temporary relief which cannot or should not be continued. Using overtime and utility personnel to boost production is an alternative that does not contribute to a permanent solution.

I 1–3: Differentiate Distinctions

In differentiating distinctions, the executive tries to solve the problem in a particular way. Obvious alternatives or solutions, requiring little differentiation, probably have already occurred to the executive group. This is true with most problems. As consideration proceeds, however, recognizable points of difference should develop between sections of a subject. These differences or divergencies are the product of differentiation, in which the executive perceives two different aspects of a subject heretofore seen as an undivided whole. A discriminating vocabulary is a substantial aid to the executive at this point.

Synonyms are words having the same or nearly the same meaning and are frequently used by executives to help differentiate distinctions. When a statement is not clearly expressed and the executive counters with a synonym, such as "Do you mean (the synonym)?" he uses an identifying technique that consumes little time. This type of question also gives evidence of listening interest.

Synonyms also help us to identify subtle distinctions between meanings. For example, the following terms are considered (in EOT) to mean Plans: purposes, decisions, agenda, standards, policies, procedures, and forecasts. Each term carries with it a distinguishing difference. Sometimes a distinction is based upon different senses of particular meanings involved. For example, "dull" and "stupid" are synonymous when describing a person but not when describing a knife.

The table following gives nouns and verbs involved in the EOT Advancement Steps with a leading synonym for each:

SYNONYMS

Verb	*Synonym*	*Noun*	*Synonym*
Expose	Reveal	Conditions	Circumstances
Develop	Create	Ideas	Alternatives
Unify	Align	Views	Opinions
Determine	Decide	Plans	Programs
Produce	Cause	Actions	Performances
Review	Scrutinize	Results	Accomplishments

In addition to synonyms, the opposites of a term are frequently used in differentiating distinctions. An opposite is an abstraction or meaning so far apart from its counterpart in implication as to seem irreconcilable with that counterpart. Opposite terms are sometimes called antonyms, differences, antitheses, and contrasts. Opposition always implies two opposite positions, and this fact may work itself into our reasoning frequently. In the table below, opposite terms are shown for the verbs and nouns used in the Advancement Steps and the Executive Considerations of the EOT Pattern:

OPPOSITES

Verb	Opposite	Noun	Opposite
Expose	Withhold	Conditions	Results
Develop	Discourage	Ideas	Facts
Unify	Separate	Particulars	Instances
Determine	Demur	Relations	Independence
Produce	Retard	Purposes	Whims
Review	Presume	Certainties	Assumptions
Identify	Misunderstand	Satisfactions	Dissatisfactions

I 1–4: *Visualize Concepts*

A concept is an idea or abstraction that exists in the mind of an individual, often combining diverse elements into one coherent pattern of thought. Skill at conceptualizing or visualizing future conditions and combinations is an essential executive ability, the requirement becoming more intense as one climbs the organizational ladder. Because higher executives are often far removed from the site of operations, they must be able to visualize what is happening as reports of unfolding events reach them.

After extensive research or investigation, concepts must be so visualized that they are devoid of details except those which are useful, typical, or generic. The sets of ideas and thoughts that are perceived as part of a unified concept concerning future conditions may then be formalized on paper as embryonic plans.

Executives visualize concepts when they identify the common characteristics in recurring situations. As control reports are submitted, they must be able to perceive the meaning of the comparisons and contrasts between estimates or intentions and the actual results.

Unless the executive is familiar with his working material, he can hardly expect to be able to visualize concepts of "what might or ought to be." One way to become familiar with material is to work with or manipulate it by identification, discussion, analysis, comparison, contrast, and evaluation. When these things are done, the executive is in a better position to conceive abstractions of a high order which will have widespread relevance to the related particulars of a situation.

In visualizing concepts, analogies are frequently useful. Analogous words are not synonymous, but serve to point out a quality or feature on which some similarity is based. Other features of things compared may be entirely different. This contrast serves to sharpen the illustration and to isolate the feature on which similarity is based. For example, the analogy of an EOT guide point to a musical note is useful in identification, but the two terms are not synonymous. Understanding of a subject becomes more definite as executive consideration and item advancement proceed. This enhancement of definiteness is needed so that the subject may be communicated between individuals.

IDENTIFYING SUBJECTS: UNIFY VIEWS

V 1–1: Recognize Individuals

Any group is made up of individuals each with his own particular personality and peculiarities. These characteristics are conditions that the executive must take into account. If he disregards them and attempts to regiment individual perspectives and interests, the unification of views may be retarded.

An individual is a single person possessing peculiarities, perspectives, and other characteristics not exactly like those of any other person. In order to get the support of others, executives must often adapt the solution to these individual views. This does not necessarily mean that the executive surrenders the objective of advancing the item, but he must find some way to recognize and utilize the sincere views of others to advantage.

In identifying subject material, the individual supplying the material may have had more direct experience or be in a better position to observe. Unfortunately, executives frequently find that the individual best fitted to clarify the subject of their inquiry may have little skill of expression and scant organization in his presentation of the information needed. Patience and help in verbalizing are necessary in this event. It is likely that one individual may contribute only part of a fuller understanding. In this case, full identification may have to be filled in by finding different segments in different places.

If the item's advancement is to be willingly supported, the executive should take notice of views which are sometimes overlooked or may need special attention. If credit is due to an individual for some accomplishment, he should be recognized. Letting him and his group know you are aware of his participation appeals to his individual pride.

V 1–2: *Share Interests*

The company represents diverse interests and values to people, and individuals place different values upon its activities. These mutually related and sometimes apparently conflicting interests form an inter-dependent pattern of relationships. The executive should be aware of these diverging and converging interest patterns if he is to unify views toward a common undertaking. If cooperating members of the group are convinced that their interests are shared by others, the company will function more smoothly and will achieve greater results.

Sharing interests is a basic part of any executive operating technique, just as it is a successful sales presentation. In unifying views behind the undertaking, it is important for the individuals to share common interests, especially as related to the undertaken item. Interests are feelings which attach value to any activity, plan, or result. These are concerns or desires that cooperating members of a group are encouraged to share. Each member is expected to join with others when accepting a portion of operating responsibility. He should seek to discourage selfish competition or efforts to claim unearned credit.

Executives should be interested in mutual identification of the subject under discussion. Each should encourage a desire to know and to expose facts that will help everyone to understand the situation. The burden should be shared, just as it is equally upon the listener to understand as it is upon the speaker to contribute to the understanding.

V 1–3: *Encourage Flexibilities*

In unifying views, executives will encourage flexibilities of views, ideas, and understandings. Anything that interferes with adaptation, alteration, or constructive change must be removed from the situation. It frequently takes conscious attention to keep the status of the advancing item flexible. An intended change which has been announced is difficult to recall or alter. A statement printed is not as flexible as one roughed out in pencil. Sometimes overaggressiveness constitutes an obstacle to flexibility. In this case, permissiveness or doing nothing may bring more flexibility into the relationship.

A person's intensity in holding a view bears heavily upon the measures required to achieve unification. Subjective certainty sometimes inter-feres with attaining objective certainty. Each member of the group, of course, is expected to take responsibility for his own objective behavior. Try as he may, no executive can be expected to overcome easily the unreasonable rigidity or opposition brought on by personal prejudices.

Flexibility permits mobility of attention to a subject. A listener unrestricted in expressing his views of a situation may be able to identify a subject more satisfactorily than one who is confined to a narrow interpretation or circumscribed topic. If the area he covers is not relevant, it can be discarded later. Firm adherence to the subject can properly come when views are better solidified. Non-directive steps help to cultivate the free, spontaneous spirit in others. The atmosphere will then be more of "talking it over" than a formal question-and-answer session.

A person trying to identify a subject frequently needs to accept tentative assumptions and half-truths in order to cast more light upon a situation, another illustration that flexibility needs to be encouraged in receiving information and ideas. One also needs to be flexible in interpreting meanings of words used by others. A word's connotation—the product of pleasant or unpleasant associations "read into" the word as a result of our past experiences—colors its interpretation. These connotations should be recognized and deemphasized where they affect identification.

Many successful salesmen are not inclined to follow statements too literally. One of the most valid aptitude tests for sales success (Test C of Series 1, Scott Mental Alertness Test) hinges on this characteristic. The average score of our most successful salesmen lies a little below midway between the highest and lowest possible scores on this test.

V 1–4: Clarify Misunderstandings

In their efforts to produce satisfactory identification through verbal expression, executives sometimes overlook the inexactness of words themselves. Each factor causing misunderstanding is individually variable. The degree of understanding depends upon the individuals' vocabulary patterns, their discriminating and expressive efforts, the independent literal meaning of the words, and the particular situation.

A misunderstanding is the lack of agreement in visualizing the same thing between two or more individuals. The misunderstanding may be applied either to the representation of the understanding or to the understanding itself. These misinterpretations or miscomprehensions are not necessarily disagreements, but unless clarified they do cause stress. When clarified they may advantageously lead to understandings and agreements. It is desirable, therefore, to explain and interpret the information at issue—to enhance its definiteness—so that no one will misconstrue the points discussed, thus eliminating confusion.

In an operating situation, discussion ordinarily proceeds until an identification defect or a misunderstanding occurs. As soon as this happens, the misunderstanding should be clarified for progress to continue. Achievement of an understanding will be evident through the use of restatements and illustrations. If individuals have been recognized, if interests have been shared, and if flexibilities have been encouraged in this part of unifying views, any remaining misunderstandings are probably legitimate and honest ones.

People occasionally simply do not try to reach a common understanding. The level of literalness plays a substantial part in these cases, and unless a favorable relations plateau is reached between individuals, logical presentation or argument bears little fruit.

When identifying questions become too pointed, sometimes aversion arises against further clarification of information. Some executives frequently are reluctant to ask identifying questions because they may feel that it reveals ignorance about a subject or situation. On the other hand, some individuals ask questions merely to demonstrate their knowledge rather than to clarify their understanding. Skillful executives sometimes keep silent until they start piecing together the meaning of a subject and then ask questions to fill out the patterns of meaning. In any case, the executive's obligation is to clarify any misunderstandings of the subjects being identified, whether others help or not. In fact, if he is being deliberately misled, he must try to sense this development and overcome it.

IDENTIFYING SUBJECTS: DETERMINE PLANS

P 1-1: Comprehend Policies

A policy is a general statement of organizational authority for guidance in deciding particular instances falling within a general category. To make a desired solution conform to company policy, at least one executive in the group must acquire an understanding of policies affecting the situation.

Policies are formulated for the purpose of guiding decisions and deal, for example, with deviations from prices, credit terms, personnel selection and compensation, and similar company affairs. Generally broad in meaning, policies guide in considering problems at a much narrower scope. Recognizing the applicability of a broad policy to a specific problem's narrower level causes the *Comprehend Policy* guide point to become useful. For example, a precedent authorized by an important decision may be followed as a policy in the future. Experience with such decisions or policies serves to indoctrinate personnel on the company's fundamental philosophy.

Some policies of an organization relate to decisions that favor economical or effective company operations. An illustration of this is the policy of setting up a national chain of warehouses to distribute products within a trade area. The decision to start producing a basically new product would also set up a fundamental operating condition. Such policies require creative development and sound judgment to be successful.

Policies may be collected for permanent reference. Certain broad guiding policies of the enterprise should be made explicit and stated as objectives, such as a policy calling for a stated sales increase every year.

Steps taken in determining plans should be consistent with general policies of the company. Some situations require effort and adaptation to stay within company policy, but adhering to the policy is generally more desirable than adopting a convenient, opportunistic solution with little regard for the future. More planning effort is needed to keep within sound policy, but it is paid back by smoother operations in the future.

A good policy for individual executives is to sharpen identification faculties and attitudes by vocabulary improvement and similar means. The executive should be capable of visualizing projected actions in generalized form so he can relate them to broader scopes of policy. In this way, he will be able to recognize possible deviations from policy and to make necessary corrections before the plan has matured too far. Certainly policy deviations should be corrected before action has been produced.

EOT discussions have proven useful at Williamson-Dickie in bringing top management policy questions before the entire executive group. Consequently the company policy and strategy become better understood by operating executives throughout the organization. These policy discussions alert junior executives to issues that require attention at a higher management level.

P 1–2: Define Objectives

An objective is an intended state of affairs, which there is an impelling, but not necessarily compelling, obligation to reach. This aim, goal, or intended result usually must be defined so that the area intended is correctly delimited and other factors excluded. Objectives of the undertaken item should be well defined if the item's title does not make the objective self-evident.

Objectives are useful instruments in executive work, becoming most relevant at the point of their identification or understanding. Careful definition reveals that objectives vary in scope, content, and type. There are, for example, broad continuing objectives. The head of a business might seek an adequate annual return on investment in the business. Within a more narrow scope, the Sales Manager might seek to produce a specific amount of sales each quarter.

Broad continuing objectives have no immediate beginning or end. Each organizational position has such objectives, continuous in nature and broad enough to encompass the entire position's authority and responsibility. The company's strategy or broad objectives may represent the full contextual scope of plans. These objectives affect the welfare of the company and the individuals connected with it.

Frequently completion objectives may involve finishing a project that has been several years in process. In such a project a series of intermediate objectives will be useful.

Defining is a traditional identifying technique and, if adequately carried out, helps establish definiteness in meaning of a term. If a definition has a pattern, then the composition and arrangement of this pattern may suggest techniques of identifying. One element of definition is category. Formal logic requires the category to be included in a definition. In this way, cow's milk is a lacteal *secretion*; cement, a calcareous and argillaceous *mixture*; or, as in EOT, conditions are *factors* existing within a situation; plans are systematic *arrangements*; results are a terminal *status*. Category as illustrated is a general class or division to which a term belongs and is more general in scope than the term being defined.

Elements other than category may be developed into the definitional breakdown scheme; for example, the quality attribute which sets apart the subject being defined from other occupants of the same category. Other factors may include the location or "where" of the activity or consideration, the function or "how" of the term, and the purpose or "why."

P 1–3: Undertake Items

Items are units of management work for executive scheduling, consideration, and handling. Although items are also known as things to do, undertakings, and projects, generally they are looked upon as "projects under way." The emphasis upon undertaken items in EOT is not intended to relieve executives of responsibility for broad continuing objectives or assigned functions. Items are merely a means to divide the opportunities for advancing these functions into definite segments. An item (in the sense we use it) has a start, an advancement (or series of advancements), and a stop.

Executives who wait for work to come to them are not as aware of the necessity of carving out items as executives who aggressively search for opportunities to create items within the framework of their responsibilities and company objectives. Being "caught up" with routine work which normally comes to them aids the executives in the creation of new items to undertake.

Undertaking the item is of course a frequent executive activity. A knowledge of conditions usually precedes the start of this step, because items arise from a situation or key issue. An item needs to be visualized in action form, and clarification of the "dramatis personae" or "who" is to handle the item helps delineate it.

There is no end to the number of things an executive could handle or the items he could undertake out of a theoretical review of his responsibilities. The difference between a results-producing item and a non-results-producing item is a key distinction before deciding to undertake an item.

A farsighted executive selects from the dozen or so items the ones on which he can most profitably spend his current time and energy. These items reflect the greatest opportunity for productive action or results in the current operating situation, hence, the importance of recognizing the situation as a first step in setting up an item.

Usually the item is visualized and declared at one level of scope. Then the scope is narrowed, and the first advancement step of Exposing Conditions is handled. This is consistent with the normal urge to expose and identify at the outset.

As the item becomes a task to perform, frequently the assignment is visualized as "the next step." Accepting the full item as an assignment, however, usually contributes to a more efficient performance.

P 1-4: *Create New Steps*

A conference aimed at advancing an item should be terminated by creating a "next step" which can be noted, filed, indexed, and later referred to. These next steps usually first appear as ideas in the form of alternative possible actions.

A next step is a segment of planned work, specific enough to be assigned and completed before a reporting or reviewing date. It usually constitutes a step in the advancement toward the item completion. Synonyms are: immediate objective, assignment, agreed next step, and colloquially at Williamson-Dickie, "A-1."

Concluding a conference or advancement effort with a next step or an assignment, ends the conference with a basis for further advancement. The Williamson-Dickie organization practiced several months in EOT sessions on concluding conferences with a next step. Agreeing on the next step coordinates members of the group around one focal scope. Its usefulness recognized, it is now a common practice in the firm.

At average operational scopes next steps usually are narrow enough to be reported upon within a week. During this interval, action on the next step should be produced. A next step, therefore, must be specific enough to handle within a short span of time. It must be quickly reducible to action status for easier assignment of accountability.

As the following case illustrates, a next step is of narrower scope than the item to which it relates. Recently our manufacturing executives became concerned about excessive variation among several plants in direct labor costs. Plant 5 was singled out as the location of the greatest opportunity for improvement. The particular cost accounting element to be studied was selected: Direct Labor Variance. The item's title thus became "Dungaree Production Direct Labor Variance."

Views were not completely unified at first. Some executives believed that tighter quality standards were causing the increase in Direct Labor Variance, while others felt that declining morale was a major cause. The executive sponsoring this issue claimed that morale would be improved if production were increased to boost employee incentive earnings. At the same time, all could agree that tighter quality standards undoubtedly affected the likely problem operations. The agreed next step, therefore, became "Select Problem Operation."

Sometimes merely creating this next step shoves the item off dead center. At other times, however, the conferring executives should create a series of "next steps," because participants may complete the first step quite soon and run out of creative work to do. In setting up such a series of next steps, managers must recognize that its sequence and validity are tentative and may be changed as later developments occur.

Creation of next steps from executive operating material is one of the skills required of all executives. The next step is the basis of the immediate group objective and the subsequent course of the undertaking.

Some items and next steps (A-1) from situations at Williamson-Dickie as they were actually set up can be found on the following pages.

Production Department

Item: Operating Expense Variance
    A1 Develop more realistic estimate on indirect labor variance. (This is an item between the Factory Manager and the Superintendent)

Personnel Division

Item: Absentee Control
    A1 Publish individuals with highest absentee rate previous month.

Item: Working Conditions
    A1 Determine reaction Press Room employees to improvement in ventilation.

Sales Division

Item: Volume Group Accounts
    A1 Develop record calls on volume accounts $15,000 and up. (Item handled by Sales Manager and Sales Office Manager)

Item: Develop Division Sales Managers
    A1 Review sales versus quota by salesmen for 1962, and develop 1963 quota. (Item between Field Sales Manager and Division Sales Managers)

Finance Division

Item: Direct Labor Cost Control
> A1   Test revised direct labor cost control sheet on one dungaree unit.
>
> (Item between Treasurer and Controller)

Item: Operating Statement Estimate
> A1   Secure department head expense estimates for balance 1962, basis Sales Estimate 8/6/62 and Production Estimate 8/6/62.
>
> (Item between Treasurer and Controller)

Research Division

Item: Point-of-Sale Advertising Survey
> A1   Tabulate and distribute survey results.
>
> (Item between Research Director and Assistant Research Director)

Item: Boys' Dungarees, 11 oz. Napped-Back Denim
> A1   Survey acceptance regular 11 oz. vs. printed napped-back 11 oz.

IDENTIFYING SUBJECTS: PRODUCE ACTIONS

A 1–1: *Conduct Pilot Experiments*

Running the full course of a cycle is usually advantageous. Sometimes, however, attempting to accomplish the first cycle on too broad a scale will hamper effective operations. Reducing the scale of operation to a narrower scope is then necessary. Completing this narrow cycle covers the full range of experience to be expected later on the broader scale.

The executive should take full advantage of feasible pilot experiments. These trial runs, tryouts, or dress rehearsals are much less expensive than full-scale installations, since they are necessarily smaller and less involved. Nevertheless, they permit a complete observation of a cycle of action, with considerably less time, risk, and energy. Because a pilot experiment will almost inevitably reveal the need for further modifications, it should be started early enough to allow careful study and revision.

The constant pressure of time and the disruption caused by installation of new manufacturing methods throughout the plant has encouraged us to reduce such projects to a pilot scale. Thus the method could be tested and proved before multiplication to a large scale operation.

To *conduct* means to use one's abilities and resources to the utmost in carrying through a complete cycle of action. The experiment should be conducted through the entire cycle to reveal all possible unforeseen circumstances that may confront the undertaking later. Hence the guide points outlined in the Produce Actions step are generally observed in conducting all pilot experiments, thereby tying in plans with actual materialization.

A 1–2: Interpret Assignments

Before an item can be undertaken, the executive must face the fact that he has a job to do, a mission to perform, and a specific objective to achieve. This objective that he is expected to attain must be well-defined. He should reflect upon the implications and meanings of the expressed assignment and objective. His understanding should be adequate to the purpose of producing worthwhile results.

An assignment is a specific task within the limits of a broader objective. If both ends are not kept in mind, wasted effort and inadequate performance are likely results. One executive function is to find and recognize the most controlling and essential implications of an agreed course of action. The executive must then concentrate upon this target. Time spent on work foreign to the central project is usually lost. Others must then spend time and energy to recover and get back on the track to results.

The reduction of planned actions in complexity and time scope through selection of specific next steps narrows one's field to a more performable scale. At the Interpret Assignments guide point those involved should interpret and clearly visualize the assignment in light of the over-all objective. When this is done, the group is more likely to concentrate upon one assignment at a time.

Recently an executive was asked to calculate the savings which could be produced by each of five alternatives. These alternatives were mechanical improvements proposed for certain machines producing our product. The executive receiving the assignment failed to interpret it properly and submitted instead a breakdown scheme of mechanical development of all our machines.

Scattering attention, time, and money frequently retards action. Sometimes, a junior executive will superimpose another line of consideration upon the original assignment. He expects those working with him to devote equal attention and emphasis to both the original and the superimposed assignment. Such a move dilutes emphasis and hampers progress upon both. A senior executive is more qualified to coordinate organizational purposes.

Occasionally, an executive sets up competing assignments, deliberately by-passing instructions. More frequently, however, this failure results from laxity in interpreting the assignment. Sometimes an executive tries to avoid distasteful chores unconsciously by putting off the needed action. To produce real action, however, he must interpret and center upon the target of the assignment.

To the executive attempting to carry it out, an assignment may appear to be purposeless or impractical. His reaction may be to question the judgment of the senior executive or his associates. Of course, there are many cases in which the events are unforeseen and unexpected. Just as frequently, however, there is a defect or inadequacy in interpretation of the assignment. The reporting executive at this point must have the capacity to differentiate this possible distinction.

Items that are easily understood and handled are generally delegated to those below the executive level. For this reason, those items reaching the executive may require more than the ordinary effort to understand and identify. If the executive seldom makes a considerable identifying effort, he may be avoiding difficult material, or his seniors may feel his identifying effort is inadequate. When difficult material is met, the executive should not be satisfied until he understands. If he is satisfied to proceed further without a full understanding, the first person misled may be himself.

In interpreting assignments, the executive is also dealing with the understanding of a subject involving others. He must align his understanding and interpretation with all concerned.

The executive needs to identify the content elements included within an assignment interpretation, just as it was necessary for him to define the item or project objectives. If the assignment is not completely identified and understood by group members, several conferences may be needed to advance the item. It also may appear that competitive projects or steps are emphasized more by certain individuals than others. These points should have been covered under such guide points as V 1–2: Share Interests and V 1–1: Recognize Individuals. In recognizing the contributions of individuals, however, there is danger of including too much material within the assignment. This, in fact, may produce competitive alternatives that interfere with team's working on first things first.

A 1-3: *Study Approaches*

Once the executive has interpreted his assignment and centered upon what he is going to do, logically he should then study how he is going to do it. He must, in short, study the immediate approaches. Approaches are introductory and immediate courses of action applicable to carrying out the details of short action cycles. The executive's purpose at this point is to produce tangible advancement of the item. He needs to pay special attention to immediate tactics, methods, or mechanics, and to be cautious in following set procedures or blind routines. Although he must keep the broad strategy intended in mind, it probably will not limit the intermediate order or sequence of steps.

The executive should study all approaches that may influence advancement in the direction of desired objectives. In studying them he fixes his mind attentively on them for the purpose of learning the possibilities, applications, and characteristics. He will examine, concentrate upon, or consider them carefully.

Most tactical steps are not decided until the situation is faced, as possible requirements to be met may be so varied that advance speculation upon alternatives would be nonproductive. But now the executive is concerned with facing immediate and impending action. He must identify present needs. The main point is that action must be started; the urge to analyze further must be restrained. His understanding and identification of the subject should enable him to select a satisfactory approach. Or the only approach available may be to start or to do something—anything! Generally, if action of some kind is started, an alternative approach will suggest itself. Through evaluation the executive may recognize and identify certain omissions in the preparation of preliminaries. Action needs to be emphasized at this point, and frequently the best way of disclosing action approaches is through action itself.

A 1-4: *Initiate Participations*

There comes a time when passive planning must halt and positive action must begin. It is the time for the executive to initiate action. He must start changes into effect that set in motion an intended course of action. As experienced executives know, about all a procrastinated project often needs is a good start. Then, when the planned events begin unfolding into reality and the dread of forging ahead into the unknown is removed, all may realize that only initiation or actuation was needed.

Elaborate plans, however, often require more from the executive than his simply deciding when action should commence. In this context the personal participation of the key executive becomes an essential consideration. In short, he must initiate action through personal participation and leadership. This participation is a personal activity which directly contributes to the solution of the item at hand. It is fundamental throughout an EOT.

The usual purpose of participation is to get the job done, but the corollary benefits are great. Each member of an executive group will personally benefit by participation, as each individual learns by doing. An individual may evaluate his own personal participation by asking himself these questions: To what extent am I satisfied with my own personal participation? Is my interest sincere? An underlying requirement is to "try for the team."

Working with an item calls for an active and balanced participation between the executives involved. An inadequately participating individual usually lacks the leadership ability which is essential to an executive's success.

To advance the undertaken item, the executive must enlist the full measure of energy, enthusiasm, and ability of all concerned toward the defined objective. To do this, he must consider the conduct and influences which bring out personal participation in others. He often participates to encourage the participation of others by contributing ideas. He brings about participation by starting, volunteering, asking identifying questions, or making counterstatements. He may ask questions, although if group members may be induced to do so, participation becomes more spontaneous. Questions posed to the leader should be answered by another member of the group if possible.

A key means of initiating participation of others is to encourage those affected by a plan of action to take part in the decision-making process. The executive still makes the decision, but his juniors participate by producing the alternatives and by estimating the probable consequences of each alternative. Closely allied to initiating participations is the executive process of delegation and assignment.

If others are to contribute their best efforts, the executive must recognize and seek to satisfy their human wants. Individuals are encouraged, for example, when their contributions are recognized or discussed. Interest signals in the group should be carefully watched.

One individual may be especially assigned to watch interest, which helps develop that individual's leadership. Some individuals are easily discouraged, and interruptions retard their participation.

Formal procedures are frequently helpful in producing group participation. The procedure for the review of item conference notes discussed elsewhere in this book has been used successfully to stimulate orderly group participation. A leader should maintain an orderly logical continuity of context.

The executive needs to be aware of the degree to which members of the group have entered into the advancement effort in the area under consideration. A well-coordinated group of freely participating individuals may require little leadership to achieve a productive level of participation. Conversely, a group of individuals who are low in participation may require skillful leadership.

The size of the group affects participation. Experience at Williamson-Dickie has indicated that about 25 in a group is a maximum number for active participation. Introductions of group members by themselves or other members help to create a favorable atmosphere for first meetings.

IDENTIFYING SUBJECTS: REVIEW RESULTS

R 1–1: Hold Conferences

A *conference* (or more particularly, an item advancement conference) is a group of individuals gathered to discuss an undertaken item. The group receives and discusses reports of item progress or advancement and sets up next steps. Item conferences usually set in motion a review of results by going over item accomplishments since the last conference. This activity is also referred to as *checking up* or *following through*.

The first conference on a new item differs from subsequent conferences because progress resulting from a previously agreed assignment or next step is not reported.

Conference discussions sometimes lead into a report of exposed conditions. It is convenient for the group to examine exposed conditions at this time. The emphasis, however, should be on reviewing results. Results not reviewed indicate a failure to follow through, signaling neglect of the item. Results are usually much easier to visualize clearly than the means used to produce them, and they frequently prove the value of a particular undertaking.

Holding item conferences, executives usually find, brings them up to date with reality and the most recent developments in the situation. All members of the executive group, as well as the senior executive, receive progress reports to achieve a greater understanding of the item and situation.

Although the senior executive typically opens the item conference, other executives may open the conference when they have interesting reports. The item conference may be initiated by either the junior or the senior executive, as both should feel responsibility to keep the item moving without undue delay.

When and how often item conferences are to be held are in themselves important considerations. Once a week is a convenient frequency; however, in many cases the next reporting date may be determined at the time the next step is agreed upon. If this is done excessively, however, scheduling too rigid to suit the needs of daily pressures may result. Reporting dates may sometimes be checked and coordinated with all concerned just a few hours before the meeting.

Sufficient time should be allowed between conferences, as a premature follow-through will find the next step only part way through the action. This discourages initiative and the handling of assignments through delegation. The senior executive should not wait too long, however, to inquire about the item's progress. Neither should he be unavailable when the junior executive desires to discuss the item, to report progress, or to secure approval of a recommended next step.

The individuals to be included in an item conference is a first point of consideration, and executives differ as to how to handle the matter. Some executives start a conference with one individual; and as the subject matter expands, other individuals who are functionally affected are brought into the conference. On the other hand, others start with a number of individuals and drop those who are not affected as the discussion progresses. It is difficult on certain items to determine at the outset who will be affected before the item is carried some distance into its cycle of advancement. In any event, it may be wise to keep the entire group together only long enough to get the perspective of the full problem.

Even seasoned executives sometimes dread to call an item conference. They may expect the conference to develop along nonproductive lines, judging from their past experiences with certain individuals involved. Some individuals, for example, customarily deviate from their assignments. Others, because of inadequate expression and organization of their information, delay reaching productive discussion, owing to the time required to reduce their reports to an understandable basis. The capable executive will overcome his misgivings and will use the item conference as an opportunity for eliminating these shortcomings.

In the event that a junior executive has the responsibility for advancing the item, he may initiate item conferences with the senior executive for the purpose of counsel and communication of progress. Although such a conference may end in an agreed next step, this is not necessarily a definite assignment from the senior to the junior, since the junior still carries the item. The main accomplishment here is the opportunity to learn and approve the course the junior is following. Both executives are assured that the intended progress is central to the item's main objective in carrying out company strategy. In some cases, therefore, the only agreed next step is the implication that the same course the junior has been following will be continued. Items handled with this degree of effectiveness are likely to be on the verge of being dropped by the senior executive from his direct responsibility.

Whether the junior or senior executive has the primary responsibility, the senior executive generally drops out of active participation in the item if reports reaching him are becoming increasingly satisfactory. This is done by lengthening intervals between conferences and by the process of delegation. The previous reporting executive then becomes the senior or reviewing executive on the item. Any further contact the senior executive has with the item may be in the nature of receiving routine communications—in itself an important executive operation.

R 1–2: Inspect Changes

As soon as action on an item begins to produce results, executives frequently note that these results are unlike those originally intended or visualized. Contrasts become sharper, connections stronger. Certain anticipated considerations have dropped out of the picture, and new possibilities have appeared that were not anticipated or correctly estimated.

As the executive leads his group into unfamiliar ground, he must bear in mind that others who have not followed the item's advancement cycle may not have a seasoned perspective for interpreting results. Much of his effort in the earlier advancement steps, therefore, should be directed toward conditioning others to expect changes.

Changes are particular differences between the current status of an undertaking and an earlier status. They are the differences or the modifications that have occurred since the previous inspection and, in fact, represent the performance during the period of effort under review.

The executive must examine these changes carefully and closely to gain information. This inspection serves a useful function, as observation of an operation will often inspire others to take greater pride in their accomplishments. Similarly, correction of deteriorations or misconceptions is desired by most employees.

The executive in an item conference may ask for particular changes within the item or situation since the last meeting. This identifying technique usually gets matters off to a quick start. He particularly seeks to distinguish or detect action without progress, a common result of misinterpretation of the assignment.

A frequent reason for changes being mere changes and not improvements is the responsible executive's lack of concentration upon the assignment because of some misinterpretation. He may indeed have accomplished a difficult task that taxed his ability as an executive. Nevertheless, the change he accomplished is not an advancement or an improvement unless it relates directly to his assigned, undertaken item.

The supervising executive should realize that he will frequently be required to discriminate between improvement and mere change. Because he cannot scrutinize all the changes taking place in an organization, the line executive will often find that inspection can be delegated as a staff function with significant advantages. The staff inspector need not interfere with the authority or responsibility of the executives whose operations he surveys. But his specialized and expert perspective will enable him to report succinctly concerning changes that occur.

R 1–3: Recall Notations

The topical contents of item conferences are generally preserved not only in the memories of executives but in notes made at the time. Notations in this context are the facts or ideas contained within the scope of a previous discussion or experience. They are an assemblage of content elements. Emphasis is generally more upon substance than upon the content form. The ability to recall notations has important implications and indicates interest, effort, and grasp with respect to a subject.

In our organization it has become customary to maintain a chronological note file in which item conference notes are entered. Each sheet of notes on 8½ x 11-inch paper is filed by date with the latest sheet on top. These bound chronological note files are frequently consulted to excellent advantage, serving as a useful adjunct to man's imperfect memory.

The extent to which busy executives should depend upon memory is not a simple question to answer. What to remember and what to forget becomes a discriminating consideration with powerful effects. Some optimal balance should be sought between overreliance and under-reliance upon memory. In striking this balance executives should note that making a reasonable effort to remember is scarcely ever injurious. Further, memory has some qualities that contrast with written memorandums. The mind has the unique advantage of random access to stored information, thereby providing much greater flexibility than written material. Memory responds with inferences and evaluations; the written page does not. The fluidity of the mind should be used to refine arrangements of our thought patterns; written notes should be depended upon to refresh our memories. In this way, each supplements the other without interference.

R 1–4: Assemble Records

To review results, relevant information must be assembled. Such information must be brought together in one place—merely knowing its whereabouts is typically insufficient for a proper review of results. Written records or other record forms containing this needed information are important exhibits, and they must be gathered or assembled for convenient reference at one time and place.

In assembling records, emphasis is placed upon written information and figures in convenient and accessible position. Missing records cause worry, but information in too many places also antagonizes the executive. Unassembled records make the course of investigation far more complex than if the information is in only one or two places.

Records and notes in understandable form can be reviewed quickly and easily. Items being handled by executives generally are important enough to be referred to and "replayed." It is desirable, therefore, that notes and other records be assembled in one place so that the executive can refer to them without checking several different sources. To integrate the information may require some copying which encourages the executive to consolidate the content highlights of the item. This is especially true when notes of several different conferences over a period of time result in an inconvenient separation of material. Alphabetical lists of the highlights or key points provide a quick reference check.

Identification of subjects must be considered at every step in advancement of an item and can not safely be limited to the specific guide points associated with each step. The experienced executive projects consideration of subjects into the action stage while developing ideas. But consideration of subjects must almost simultaneously involve consideration of the particulars of the situation and how they may be expressed for executive attention.

FIGURE 5.

PROCEDURE FOR REVIEW OF
ITEM CONFERENCE NOTES

STEPS *		KEY POINTS	
1	Review item title entered in note files of individuals involved in item conferences.	101	Is the item title brief, six words preferable. (6 or less)
	See if all individuals involved write the item title in their note files. (Yes)	102	Does it express the complete sense as to the:
		1021	Scope of the item? (Yes)
		1022	Objective to be reached. (Optional)
		103	Are the views of the individuals aligned as to the:
		1031	Scope of the item? (Yes)
		1032	Objective of the item? (Yes)
11	Identify and enter chairman of the item. (Yes)	1101	Does the chairman of the item have an item card in his Schedufile, notes in the margin of his Chronological Note File, or a list of items? (Yes)
12	Enter any reports, communications, and approvals of the item. (Yes)	1201	Does the item present a change in company policy? If so, has it been cleared with the proper authority? (Yes)

* Desirable answer (in parenthesis) follows each step or key point.

STEPS *		KEY POINTS	
2	Review next steps entered in note files of individuals involved in item conference. (Yes)	201	Extent of next step should be no broader than what can be finished before next reporting date? (O. K.)
	See if individuals who are to review the report as well as those who are to advance the next step and report have written the next step in their note files. (Yes)	202	The step after the next step is not the next step unless it is part of an agreed sequence. (O. K.)
		203	Alternative possible next steps are not next steps, but are ideas. (O. K.)
21	Every item conference should terminate with an agreed next step. (Yes)	2101	Ideas and plans—cross fertilize contributions.
		2102	Alternatives help in determining next step.
		2103	Analyzing the item and the material helps in developing alternatives.
22	If any next step is indefinitely expressed, identify area in the notes considered to be next step. (O. K.)		
3	Where more than one next step involves more than one person, the responsible persons should be identified by initials or otherwise. (Yes)	301	Reviewing chairman should be senior to individuals agreeing to handle and report on the next step. (Yes)
	Identify both those who review the report and those who advance and report next step.		
	Where more than one next step is agreed to by one person, each step should be identified separately. (One or Yes)		
5	Where next steps are to be done in chronological order, the sequence should be identified. (None or Yes)	501	The sequence noted by the Reviewing Chairman or executive is the controlling sequence.

* Desirable answer (in parenthesis) follows each step or key point

STEPS *   KEY POINTS

6   Reminder notes to yourself
    should be identified with ini-
    tials or otherwise. (None or
    Yes)

7   An agreed next step should be   701   Assignments should be spe-
    accepted or modified before   cific enough to be next
    the conference ends and not   steps. (Yes)
    afterward. (Yes)

                                           702   Some sub-items are broader
                                                  than next steps and should
                                                  not be considered as next
                                                  steps. (O. K.)

                                           703   Are views of individuals in-
                                                  volved aligned as to the ob-
                                                  jective of the next step?
                                                  (Yes)

    If a next step is modified after
    a conference, communicate
    with other individuals involved
    before modification. (None
    or O. K.)

    Enter follow-up reminder on
    margin of note file or item
    card. (None or Yes)

* Desirable answer (in parenthesis) follows each step or key point.

V

Expressing Particulars

Expressing particulars is the presentation of information so that it may be communicated between two or more individuals. For communication to be complete, there must be both adequate expression and impression of the material communicated. In expressing particulars emphasis is upon expression for transmittal in understandable form. The impression received is usually considered in the reciprocally related activity of identifying.

All types of executive material are transmitted in expressing: satisfactions, subjects, relations, results, ideas, views, plans, and particulars. In fact, the EOT guide points themselves represent categories of information commonly expressed as particulars.

Expression does not necessarily have to be verbal to be effective. Exhibits and demonstrations are frequently more potent than either oral or written expressions. A proposition presented in narrative or story form, indirectly expressing the point intended, is also effective.

Because the aim of expression is to be unmistakably understood, definiteness is required. A statement may be definitely expressed without necessarily being accurate. Figures are examples of definite expressions. An executive who expresses a particular concept usually must first understand it. The expression then may be extended into teaching, training, or coaching those who report to him. Telling, showing, and getting the receiver to demonstrate his understanding to the executive are all required in the consideration of expressing particulars.

An individual usually relies on words to express visualized logical relationships. He already possesses his own vocabulary and a lexicon of favorite expressions. Providing a common executive vocabulary is a major aim in the EOT program.

A desire to express a point precisely and perfectly should not keep an individual from withholding an expression. The best expression available is better than no expression. On the other hand, most people have a natural desire to express their understandings. Sometimes they become absorbed in the sound of their voices and overemphasize expression at the expense of identification.

The ability to express is commensurate with the ability to understand. Expressing is frequently more easily handled if the content elements are gathered piecemeal before any attempt is made to arrange them into form or sequence. After the executive has "moved the furniture into the room," so to speak, he can arrange it by sequencing the particulars. Recognition of the relationships among the content segments forms as familiarity increases.

Lengthy expressions require additional interest-holding factors, such as examples from actual experience, suspense, insufficiencies, needs, challenges, situations, or narrative and chronological forms.

A particular is a single entity which exists as the only one of its class. If reproduced, it will exist as another particular, possibly belonging to the same general class. Executive Operations discriminates between particular facts and generalizations. Just as the lawyer must distinguish between facts and inferences, the executive must visualize these particular content elements of his material. Each particular exists individually and apart from the generalizations to which it relates.

Concrete expression of particulars enhances a subject in definiteness. When the executive points out a particular feat existing within a situation currently under consideration, he is expressing particulars. He recognizes a current reality, not simply an abstraction. Delving into particulars is sometimes unpleasant for it disturbs the executive's preconceptions and inconveniences his rationalizations. Nevertheless, it supplies an opportunity for alignment with reality and sets the stage for advancement of an item.

C 2–1: *Describe Understandings*

Understanding is the first evolutionary step toward adequate expression. After grasping the meaning of a subject, the executive usually must verbally describe his understanding so that it may be communicated or preserved. The statement thus is a representation in his own words of this segment of content; that is, a description of his understanding of the subject.

When an executive states his understanding of a subject, he is expressing particulars. When listening, he frequently describes his understanding by summarizing the statements made to him with the question "Is that what you mean?" Although such a question is a direct example of formulating an expression, his purpose may be to identify the subject. Frequently the other individual restates the particular in different words, starting with "No, this is what I mean." In this way the expressions tend to become increasingly clear, brief, and adequate for the purpose in mind.

Describing and explaining are synonymous. A frequently observed precaution in executive operations is that one must describe before evaluating. Evaluation differs from merely describing. Describing entails no more than selecting words and framing expressions of a visualized understanding.

An intercommunicating group uses a terminology of its own. Individuals who have mastered this group vocabulary pattern "talk the language," making their expressions more understandable.

The first responsibility for mutual understanding should be taken by the speaker. He should align the literal meaning of what he says with the intended meaning of his statement. Not being sufficiently literal in expression and being too literal in impression can cause problems. Executives when listening need to focus both upon the literal statement as well as what the other individual may actually mean. A group relationship of long standing may be informal and may interpret and receive statements less literally than a new group relationship.

Single words used as synonyms or opposites convey meaning and add understanding. These words represent relatively simple units of comprehension. Statements also are used in identifying and form a less simple pattern. A statement made for the purpose of conveying the complete meaning of a term is called a definition. Definitions have been discussed in Chapter IV under P13, Define Objectives.

C 2–2: *List Contents*

Exposure of conditions is more effective if information is presented in written statements. These separate pieces of information called *content elements* are important in executive operations. They are the topical segments of the situation with which the executive is dealing. At the time of exposure, content elements lie fresh and vivid in the executive's memory. But unless notes are kept, they may fade as time and new disclosures overlay them. For this reason executives need to list the contents of a particular situation upon a record. Then this entry may be read, understood, and later referred to. Executives learn to condense notes to telegraphic brevity.

Making notes or listing is a tangible foundation for future executive operations and is evidence of item advancement efforts and work done in the past. Making notes is an activity under the personal control of each executive. When he exhibits the initiative of making notes of conditions, ideas, and next steps, the executive encourages the confidence of others. He indicates the capacity for noting independently what needs to be done. He imparts a feeling of assurance that he will follow through on these notes with effective action.

If plans are misunderstood or deviated from, the literal notes supplement memory. Recording and indexing such notes for convenient reference is a desirable requirement in most executive work.

Content elements are segments of information that become the basis for reasoning for a solution. They are especially useful for inductive reasoning. Content elements frequently are exposed conditions or carried-over known facts. Although generally substantive, they may be definite or procedural elements. These elements are not fully acquired or collected until the executive records or lists them.

As the material involved in an intensive project increases in volume, other techniques may be needed in order to keep it manageably arranged. An alphabetical listing is simple and automatic and requires no classification—merely exposure, selection, and entry. The sequence is random and automatic. With no more than approximately 36 content elements on one page, the collection is usually suited to numerical sequence. Numerical arrangement seems to be a natural step, following a random or alphabetical arrangement.

One advantage of a simple, linear sequence is that the executive need not be concerned with variation in generality levels of the elements listed. His sense of order guides him to put a general term ahead of a series of subordinated terms. Even though these different levels of generality are recognized, the arrangement still has not extended beyond one dimension.

In constructing a representation of desired plans, as in any other process, basic units are helpful. Material may be blocked out from the continuous ribbon of experience in the form of situations, items, considerations, possible actions, or content elements of situations.

The existence of a content list helps executive operations. Generally a list is made flexible; for example, it is first written in pencil and later is made more rigid for publication in typewritten or printed form. The initial random or chronological listing also permits spontaneous mental association. Chronological order of occurrence is a satisfactory way to preserve the list for later use. Experience with chronological note files, as contrasted with previously used classified files, indicates this.

Executives sometimes assume a situation is simpler than it is. Apparently, in trying to save time, they endeavor to simultaneously collect content material elements, list them in serial order, and develop a two-dimensional arrangement. Confusion frequently results when a mass of material has no order. Even worse, the elements may be in a partially ordered and incomplete arrangement, an arrangement which will probably need dissolving before it is flexible enough for rational organization.

C 2–3: *Figure Costs*

Every operation in business (and in life itself) entails some costs. The business executive must be attuned to these costs inherent in all his work, for nothing can be accomplished without paying a price, enduring a sacrifice, or sustaining some sort of loss. To attain an end, a variety of costs must be encountered in the process.

Not all costs lend themselves to numerical expression, but those that can be stated as *figures* usually are most helpful in deciding between alternative courses of action. These figures can be used to reckon, compute, and compare as the final solution to a problem is sought.

Figures are symbols representing a quantity or successive arrangement of particulars, usually expressed in a definite number of units. Figures are also known as statistics, or units of inventory, or activity. Information which can be reduced to and supplied in figures is more easily understood when communicated to others.

To be susceptible to numerical expression, information needs to have a serial, spatial, quantitative, or magnitudinous characteristic. Before figures can be effectively used, countable or measurable entities must be available. In addition, a suitable unit must be selected.

The executive must be aware of the distinction between the particular entity which the unit represents (for example, the fourteenth machine) and the single abstract term of unit which may represent it (for example, fifteen Type X machines). Mathematicians and others distinguish between these types of numbers by using the terms cardinal and ordinal. Cardinal numbers are *one, two, three*, etc., in distinction from *first, second, third*, etc., which are called ordinal numbers.

Many accounting costs can be readily figured and reduced to comparable terms. Accountants are usually versed in cost accounting, and all executives should know at least the rudiments of these techniques. Rough approximations of relative costs must often be made in advance of detailed analyses by staff specialists.

The implicit cost of choosing among several alternatives also must be figured. This cost is often known as *opportunity cost*, a figure representing the difference in net returns from alternative business decisions. One alternative may indeed return a profit, but among its implicit costs are the dollars not earned or sacrificed as a result of choosing the least profitable alternative. This is one cost figure that must never be overlooked.

C 2-4: Supply Exhibits

In law, an exhibit is a document or material object that can be used as evidence in supporting a contention. Just as attorneys use exhibits, so executives can use them to advantage as a part of their operating technique.

Models, charts, or samples used as exhibits frequently tell a more complete story than words or figures alone. If the executive has such an exhibit to supply his audience, his description of particulars is frequently more effective, since most people like to be shown as well as told. A model or drawing which stands in place of a proposed method encourages more definite exposure of conditions. Check lists and procedures frequently help illustrate conditions. Case illustrations and information presented in narrative form frequently add interest and effectiveness, even in a formal presentation.

EXPRESSING PARTICULARS: DEVELOP IDEAS

I 2–1: Suggest Recommendations

A recommendation is a statement or piece of advice offered for use or consideration by others. Executives are encouraged to suggest recommendations as an effective technique for developing organizational teamwork. This is especially important in increasing junior executives' initiative without decreasing that of senior executives, thus broadening the base of participation. Senior individuals encourage initiative when they seek recommendations and make notes of suggestions that may be used as opportunities. This will cause fewer junior executives to withhold or reserve their recommendations.

Management thinking is evidenced by an executive's analyzing a problem sufficiently to express it as a recommendation. A recommendation should be thought through with considerable definiteness and should not be a half-baked suggestion which someone else is expected to refine to action status. An effective, creative relationship between executives encourages both the giving and receiving of recommendations. It is their responsibility to improve on ideas received on the same subject rather than to change the subject.

When an executive makes a recommendation, his ideas become tangibly useful. Many times executives have good ideas but withhold them for some reason. With Dr. Eliot Chapple's aid we measured the proportion of contacts initiated by junior and senior executives in 1949 and again in 1952. The proportion initiated by juniors in the interim increased substantially.

Sometimes it is better to err on the side of initiating early action rather than to stress too heavily the requirement of checking with everybody. Generally, however, it is better to emphasize initiative at the recommendation phase and to refrain from acting without communicating. Executives who wait to be told what to do frequently do not deserve to be called executives. Executives who are skilled in suggesting recommendations wait for openings when the time is appropriate and offer the suggestions when they will count the most. Many times suggestions are sought and made for their cross-fertilization usefulness.

I 2–2: *Calculate Ratios*

Executives frequently need to express information in the form of ratios. Reducing data to precise terms by expressions such as ratios will sometimes make an imposing question less difficult to decide. Comparisons in terms of a common denominator are objective, concise, and convincing. Their precise objectivity epitomizes the executive consideration of *Expressing Particulars*.

Formal training in mathematics, statistics, accounting, and engineering increases the ability to use and understand ratios. Even without this training, however, the competent executive can develop skills in calculating ratios to measure performance by comparing intentions with results. The most significant portions of a large business firm's operating statements are often stated as ratios. If meaningful, these ratios provide insight into the firm's operating efficiency and financial condition as no other measures can.

Ratios and percentages obviously belong in the same category. For example, the percentage of a plant's productive efficiency may be expressed as 89 per cent or 102 per cent. The ratio of each to 100 per cent is taken into consideration. Deviations from some standard can be expressed in the same way. In another application, ratios may be used to express the relative composition of the whole; total costs may include 60 per cent material costs and 40 per cent labor costs.

Comparative magnitudes are often emphatic in themselves. But when changes between magnitudes are stated in percentage terms, the extent of the change becomes far clearer. For example, if the finished goods inventory position on March 1 was 6.4 weeks' supply, and the expected position for April 1 is 2.4 weeks' supply, then the ratio of 6.4 to 2.4 represents a significant decrease in inventory level. More explicitly, the inventory decrease is 62 per cent—a pronounced rate of change expressed precisely.

Dealing with ratios, proportions, and percentages frequently suggests ideas. Calculations of this sort produce many opportunities for worthwhile manufacturing decisions. Such was the case when a review of a week's sales revealed that boy's elastic-back denim slacks were selling in substantial volume, even more than the regular make tan khaki twill pants. The question considered was this: Is the make (regular or elastic-back) more influential in the sale of boys' pants than the cloth (khaki or denim)? The only way we could determine this with certainty was to make elastic-back pants from tan khaki as well as denim and then compare the ratios of elastic-backs sold in each fabric. The ratios resulting from these calculations suggested that increasing production of the elastic-back make would be a good idea.

I 2-3: *Multiply Applications*

Applications are instances of using techniques, methods, or facilities that have been proven out in use. They may have been employed during some previous situation or during a pilot run conducted within the present situation. Expansion into greater use through multiple applications is typical of the gradual development one encounters in executive operations.

Executives often improve a situation by applying an improved method, but not always do they broaden their visualizations to include a company-wide application. In fact, this multiplication is sometimes left to other executives and becomes a different and broader cycle. There is, nevertheless, the need for a tie-in between the proof of the solution and the multiplying of its application. Here again teamwork becomes necessary in putting into effect the proved solutions so that they will not expire through nonuse or neglect.

A senior executive can multiply his time and effort by assignment to a junior executive without a loss in skill. After a thirty-minute conference between these two individuals, a next step may be developed which may take from two to ten hours of the time available to a junior executive or members of his organization. This allows the senior executive at the same time to apply his knowledge and skill to other areas. When the junior executive can demonstrate effectiveness in taking initiative at a larger scope than the detailed assignments, he multiplies the senior executive's time even more.

When an idea appears to be useful after application in one or a number of similar instances, it may then be susceptible to multiplication. Many ideas are warmed-over applications previously applied in similar situations. More narrowly many ideas are revived inclinations with regard to the current problem. Frequently it appears that nothing is new in itself, but the new application is highly useful.

The possibility of multiple applications leads into standardization and simplification, multiplying the positive conditions favorable to success. The successful executive aggressively searches for these multipliers, extending their successful application to wider areas within the enterprise. This is exemplified in the adage, "Make money first by working oneself, then other people, and finally one's dollars." Executives multiply manpower, machines, money, and markets.

I 2–4: Formulate Measurements

A measurement is a standard intended to represent the quantitative extent of an actual body or entity. A measurement is mathematical in nature, and deals with number units. In this way, distance, extent, volume, duration, magnitude, intensity, number, frequency, and weight are measured and expressed. Measurement is facilitated by instruments such as tapes, containers, and counters. This helps ascertain and express the quantitative nature of particulars. Measurements may also be made by comparison among particulars.

To *formulate* means to express in a formula or reduce to a formula. A measurement formula requires a unit such as a dollar value, pair, foot, or pound.

Measuring operating results is handled by accounting for activities and inventories. Measuring the results of the advancement of an undertaken item, however, is distinctly more difficult. A chronological step in the course of progression between start and completion may indicate a measure of item advancement.

EXPRESSING PARTICULARS: UNIFY VIEWS

V 2–1: Submit Propositions

A proposition differs from a mere recommendation. In submitting propositions, the executive seeks to gain clearance and support for a desired course by advising others of his intentions in advance. Such a proposal is usually submitted directly.

The purpose of this step is to present a proposal in such a way that it may be understood, accepted, and approved as an undertaken item for final planning. The material should be presented in an orderly, understandable form. The listener should not have to reorganize the proposition because it has been inadequately thought through. An effective procedure is to first assemble the content in random or alphabetical order. Following this, the material may be tentatively sequenced for review and later presentation.

Propositions might in formal circumstances make up an agenda, a list of topics, or proposals intended to be considered or acted upon in a conference. This may be the first time the incipient undertaking becomes outlined into expressive tangibility. Here a program is laid before others for consideration and judgment. These propositions are submitted so that those involved may discuss them for the purpose of unification of views.

Certain views influence the submission of propositions. The executive should have confidence in his propositions, and it is reasonable for him to expect normal, favorable attention to them.

V 2–2: Reveal Positions

Positions are conclusions reached by individuals about matters. These individual opinions, however, have not necessarily been stated or disclosed, and it is important in unifying views that all relevant positions be revealed to others. If positions are withheld, a valuable aspect of the undertaking may not be discovered until considerable time and effort are expended. Each person should realize that no other individual shares his perspective, and that the group needs to know the position of all its members.

Intensive, full discussions, in which executives get everything "off their chests," are more effective than meetings in which executives are on the defensive, trying to cover up, and giving evasive, defensive, or indirect answers. Views should be constructive and sincere. If a dissenting individual tries to offer a more useful alternative than the one proposed, this will keep the relationship on a positive level. Prejudices, antipathies, and attachments are all to be expected, and should be dealt with. Logical inconsistencies sometimes may remain unresolved, and objective measurements—however desirable—may not be available.

In Exposing Conditions, the critical attitude may be emphasized, but in Unifying Views, criticism should be de-emphasized. It is implied that expressed views are sincere, although mere lip service should be recognized when it becomes evident.

Occasionally positions may be ascertained indirectly in spite of executives' unwillingness to reveal their positions directly. A leading industrial engineer sometimes asked applicants, "Do you think Time Magazine's political policy is to the right or left?" Responses were clues to the applicants' attitudes.

Views are sometimes revealed by what an individual omits from what he has said. In such cases the incomplete parts frequently may be filled in by a person with knowledge of the situation and individual.

Views are frequently reflected in the individual's responsibility for the soundness of his factual position and the consistency of his logical position. Defensive rationalization through logically false statements is relatively more frequent among the highly sophisticated. Statements expected to be received as factually correct, yet made without the speaker's taking responsibility for their correctness are resorted to as defensive measures more frequently among the unsophisticated.

Each particular organization has a current level or standard of operating adequacy; and techniques which are appreciated one year may because of improved operations cease to seem important the next. One such point of this type is the defensiveness of individuals caused by more searching inquiries as a result of EOT emphasis. Executives must be conditioned to accept the responsibility for their factual and logical positions.

V 2–3: Introduce Data

Facts or figures relevant to the situation must often be brought into consideration. This factual material becomes the objective support on which others justify their conclusions.

Each individual should edit the data he is introducing. If one executive presents arguments, assumptions, and ideas in greater proportion than facts, some other executive must sift out this nonuseful material. If each executive bears this in mind, time will be saved and the material dealt with will have much more objective forcefulness.

An executive should be alert to defensiveness on the part of his associates. If defensiveness develops, he should try to modify it. One way to do this is to ask the defensive individual for facts supporting his position. Then the executive carrying the responsibility for unifying should receive these facts openly and constructively. In many cases the defensiveness of the other individual will lessen. At certain times, however, this defensiveness does not dissolve quickly, and possibly the meeting should be postponed until a more suitable time when atmosphere and emotions are more favorable for objective consideration of data.

V 2-4: *Offer Reasons*

If the executive offers the reasons he used in arriving at a conclusion, others may use them in arriving at their own conclusions. Thus others secure the advantage of his factual reasoning seeing how he evaluated and related certain facts. Defects in the logical premises of his position as well as that of others may be revealed.

Reasons are factors relevant to a situation which would logically be taken into consideration in determining conclusions and which are also important for others to hear. They should be offered so that valid contributing factors can be recognized and irrelevancies or nonuseful argument can be made evident.

EXPRESSING PARTICULARS: DETERMINE PLANS

P 2-1: *Write Details*

At this point in Expressing Particulars, details of the plan must be specified and written down. They need to be visualized precisely and definitely described or named. It is not enough for them to be implied, generally referred to, or equivocally indicated, since they must later serve as reminders in producing action. A popular misconception is that executives should not pay attention to details. Executives must pay attention to details that would otherwise be overlooked.

Details are features of a narrower scope than the major topic but of sufficient importance to require definite consideration. They are specifics but not necessarily trifles. Sometimes they are high-value specifics, as in the case of a defective upholstery fastener which may prevent an automobile dealer from selling a $5,000 car.

The amount of detail required is an important consideration. If the executive overspecifies detail and includes much unnecessary or irrelevant material, someone must edit and weed out such material. The responsible executive anticipates the details that need to be written down, in order to forestall others choosing wrong alternatives. Suggesting details to specify and write should be balanced between junior and senior executives. Otherwise, the senior executive may be drawn into the trap of doing the thinking for the juniors. Writing details gives the executive an opportunity to examine the complete list for sufficiency and adequacy.

Many executives tolerate the inconvenience of inadequately expressed particulars without taking action to improve it. Expressions may be improved either in small packages or large ones. Once the executive gets into the spirit of expressing, he will be able to remove psychological blocks and acquire the habit of writing down details. He need not be satisfied until the expression is self-sufficient without verbal supplement. Questions suggested by guide points to test the purpose of actions and usefulness of operating material will help specify these details.

Details are not adequately specified unless they are written down, and they need to be expressed with clearness and brevity. If the executive carrying out a plan is required to clarify or alter a large percentage of the details before taking action, he is moving back in the cycle to reprocess the plan before producing action.

Details recorded in a note file maintained for the purpose usually are easily understood. The entry of the item, the next step, and some clues to the objective appear in the notes of the reviewing executive as well as the reporting individuals.

A successful executive need not write details unnecessary to successful performance, as such details may be carried along with the general content of the undertaking and filled out by the productive acts which unfold. In this case the performing or reporting executive makes note of the details as they are disclosed as a part of a teamwork operation. More definite terminology or better arrangement of content may be attempted after a decision is reached.

P 2–2: Designate Titles

A title is a word or phrase by which something is distinguished or familiarly known. Executive operations are less confusing if titles are designated before the force of circumstances requires it. Organizational handling is facilitated if a subject coming into general consideration is supplied with a single symbol or name by which it may be referred to later. Even though time and thought are required, advance designation of titles avoids having the same subject referred to by several different titles which mislead or confuse.

One test of a title is: Does it express the central sense of the subject? It should also be brief and should not duplicate another title. Terms as well as names are included in the "title" category. Trademarks and slogans are examples of titles in a more advanced status.

Executives need to be aware of the effect on executive operations of entities with no titles or with inadequate, misleading titles. The title of "Production Planning Estimate of Transition from Actuals to Sales

Department Estimate" appeared on one of our reports. This title was intended to represent an immediate sales estimate made by the Production Planning Department, taking into consideration recent actual sales experience. This more current status was more useful in immediate production planning than earlier, less accurate estimates. The literal title of the new estimate did not signify the central meaning of the information reported. A more descriptive title might have been "Revised Sales Estimate Based on Current Actuals."

P 2–3: Estimate Expectations

Expectations are actions or results looked for in the future with reasonable justification. These forecasts or predictions are not necessarily brought about or influenced by the executive. They may be merely an anticipation of a result influenced by expected circumstances. Anticipated results may be sales estimates, expense budgets, or changes in general economic conditions. Good operations technique requires that expectations be estimated in advance. If expectations are not estimated, results cannot be compared and evaluated.

Estimating is concluding from speculation, reasoning, and calculating the outcome of future activities in terms of quantity, quality, or results. Such goals, estimates, or budgets are neither guesses nor retrospections; they are definite, anticipated, and forecasted expectations made with careful thought and effort.

Questions such as the following all lead to estimating expectations:

Do you have any results planned on this item?

What are they?

What is the unit?

What are the figures in terms of unit activity? of unit inventory?

P 2–4: Design Forms

Executives frequently need to express expected results in terms of goals or budgets, such as sales, expense, and production estimates. The form in which these planned results are stated is generally the same as the one used for stating the actual results.

A form in EOT is an arrangement of content or material designed to present information so that details of this information in whole and in part can be clearly and easily seen. In addition to titles, columns, and lines, the format may provide for figures, descriptions, illustrations, and other expressive devices. A form helps one see relationships, as well as the entire situation. A carefully studied and structured arrangement guides in placing kinds of information so it can be conveniently recorded, reviewed, and compared. It guides the entry and consideration of facts and figures along the lines so constructed.

Roughing out a form in a tentative and flexible manner is usually advisable at the early stages, so that everyone involved may contribute to the content, sequence, and arrangement. Sharing responsibility for the orderliness of the forms and methods of presentation is evidence of effective executive teamwork.

Many times consideration needs to be given to one uniform arrangement of information between divisions of the company such as Sales and Production. Designing forms for company-wide budgeting controls in which the activity goes beyond the capacity and control of a single individual usually justifies considerable time and effort.

In controlling the certainty of results a suitable form is necessary to express results and to provide for estimates to be compared with actuals. After the form is roughed out and test figures are entered, the designer frequently finds that extra columns are needed or that sequence needs to be rearranged.

Forms designed and filled in before putting plans into action make reporting more orderly and convenient. In designing forms to receive the consideration they deserve, distinguishing the form itself from the information to be reported is frequently helpful. Executives sometimes become so absorbed with the task of accurately completing figures to a particular period that they place little value on the form. When they emphasize the form first and then use the material primarily to test out the form, the form is more likely to be adequately designed.

EXPRESSING PARTICULARS: PRODUCE ACTIONS

A 2–1: Explain Intentions

As action progresses, other individuals become involved, and it is desirable that executives "put their cards on the table" and explain their intentions clearly.

Intentions are future courses of action which an individual has in mind before starting action. These designs or intended actions should be explained to those affected and re-explained if necessary. Explaining makes an expressed meaning understandable to others. This is done to eliminate or reduce confusion, doubts, and suspicions.

Explaining intentions may give one an opportunity to test whether the start is being made with adequate forethought. When we ask, "How are you going to carry out the step?" we have a chance to test what may happen. Explaining intentions frequently leads into particularizing the form of activity inventory, such as *shipped, received, back-ordered,* or *delayed.*

A 2–2: Follow Reminders

Reminders are written points of information which may be referred to for the purpose of refreshing memory. They are procedures, formulas, entries, or references which are available for use and guidance. Executive teamwork is easier when executives follow these reminders. Through this activity they maintain a reasonable and effective connection between guiding intentions and the process of their realization. In this an executive is encouraged to observe, pursue, or stay with a previously determined plan, not disregarding or losing sight of it. If these reminders of subject matter or plans are properly structured, they will have a real effect on the interest, economy of effort, and operating effectiveness of an executive group.

Intelligent interpreting and following of plans is an essential consideration when teamwork production of results is required. If no progress is made by subsequent reporting conferences, reminders of plans have usually not been followed properly. One reason why plans are not followed is that emphasis is not maintained on completing the agreed next step. A new alternative may have been found rather than the one agreed upon, and preoccupation with this new alternative prevents completion of the assignment.

Check lists are examples of reminders which executives frequently use. A review of a check list may be a reminder to consider all listed phases of a subject.

In following reminders it is desirable to preserve a flexibility and naturalness and to combine, if possible, the formal and literal with the informal and practical. Alertness to imperfections of plans as inevitably revealed by experience is a fundamental EOT practice.

On the other hand, the faithfulness with which reminders are followed affects their usefulness. In fact, if one abandons a procedural path, much and sometimes all of its effectiveness is lost or, at least, hindered.

Sometimes when reminders seem to hinder, executives "panic," jump the track, and free-wheel, ignoring all reminders. This may occur when the situation is too complex for the time allotted. In such cases the executive may need to shift to a simpler or more immediate scope to simplify the confusing situation.

A 2-3: Apply Formulas

Formulas are guidance schemes which direct an executive in the production of an answer. Formulas may be used repeatedly, although the particulars in each case of their application may be different. Solutions frequently require a mathematical expression susceptible to the construction and use of formulas. Application of such formulas is helpful to get action off dead center and keep it advancing.

To *apply* means to make serviceable use of something as an instrumentality; that is, to follow a previously formulated guidance scheme in carrying out a calculation or a program of action. Synonyms are: to employ, to utilize, or to use.

Formulas belong to the same general family as reminders, but they are generally proven and tested. They are not employed with the tentativeness of reminders. Formulas are guides or techniques which are definitely put into practice. They suggest action needed for answer. The formula, if applied, usually results with the expression in final and definite form.

The development and the use of the formula has been described by Professor A. R. Towl as "getting useful generalizations." The applying of the formula has also been expressed as "applying generalizations usefully." His chart of this process is shown on the following page.

A 2-4: Complete Answers

An answer may be completed on any question in which the available information is reasonably susceptible to yielding an answer. Expressing our intended results completely with mathematical precision helps focus the efforts of all concerned upon this one common, tangible goal.

The first requirement in finding an answer is to have available all of the answerable material; in other words, the ascertainables or disclosures. Incomplete material or mere inquiries will not permit a complete con-

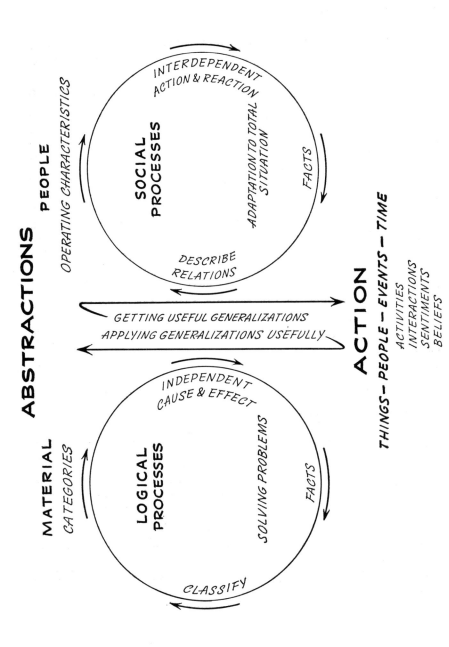

FIGURE 6. GETTING AND APPLYING USEFUL GENERALIZATIONS.

clusion. To complete is to carry an undertaking to the point that its desired usefulness is realized—to finish or conclude, rather than to leave unfinished.

To determine progress on an apparently growing stack-up of work in the factory, it is necessary to know the number of pieces on hand, the output of pieces in a given period of time being taken from the stack, and the input of pieces being put into the stack. If one of these three points of information is missing, the executive may find it very difficult to express the progress he is making on the situation. He may ask the question, "What progress are you making with regard to that stack-up in Department X?" The reply may be, "There are 1,100 pieces in the stack-up (at 9:00 o'clock) and 400 per hour are going into the stack, and 300 per hour are coming out." This obviously consists of only the ingredients from which an answer is calculated. The formula for securing the answer has not been applied. Executives who aim to produce action must carry their answers as nearly to a final conclusion as the information available permits. In the example above, the complete answer would be: "The stack-up is growing at the rate of 100 per hour. Utility personnel or some other means may be used until the stack-up is eliminated."

EXPRESSING PARTICULARS: REVIEW RESULTS

R 2–1: *Ascertain Actuals*

An *actual result* is the materialized result after action has happened. It is distinguished from a mere anticipated result. The actual result is a consciously sought advancement or gain. Nonadvancements, dead centers, or losses are also actuals, but they are not favorable actual performances. In reviewing results especially when satisfaction is considered, executives endeavor to ascertain actual results. To *ascertain* is to seek and discover information about something, to find out, to learn, or to determine.

Executives usually have available estimates or out-dated actuals from previous dealings. But the recently materialized, current, actual result may not be available without an effort. Unless the executive realizes this inequality between the actual and the estimate, he may fail to compensate between them and attach insufficient value to the actual.

To a skilled executive, the current, materializing actual results take realistic precedence over previously made estimates. This shift in perspective or point of view is essential to executive operations. Actual results affect merchandising. They should be taken into account in control of manufacturing and expense variances. If the executive is satisfied with nonactuals and if he tolerates outdated actuals, he is handicapped by not possessing an adequate representation of the current results.

R 2–2: *Record Activities*

Activity, the successive occurrence of events or the frequency with which certain units experience change, is a countable fact with which executives must reckon.

Activities are experiences, performances, or actions produced. They are measurable by counting the number of such activity units produced within a given period of time. They are frequently used to express the particulars of results. Activities such as production, output, operations, or performances are recorded in terms of number of units.

To *record* is to enter information on paper for later reference and review. Records furnish written evidence or documents that are more reliable than memory or oral reports. They are also more permanent and are transferable. Definiteness is gained if most of the results are expressed through records. Reviewing is affected by the convenience in which results are expressed.

To record activities, representative figures or valid units must be available. This does not mean, however, that sampling used in statistical quality control and other statistical techniques are not acceptable. This means that representative areas of the total operation or sample statistics representative of the total frequently are selected and used, saving considerable time and effort.

R 2–3: *Count Inventories*

Closely connected with the activity of executive events is inventory. The supply of material, the magnitude or extent all involve this quantitative determination of the number of units existing at a given time.

An inventory is a detailed list of the kind and quantity of articles on hand at one location on a particular date. It is the enumeration, the quantity on hand, or the supply.

In understanding results, it is useful to draw a distinction between activity and inventory. In Williamson-Dickie's production field, activities include all operations such as cutting, sewing, and pressing. The result of the production activity is a count of the garments moving past the last operation. The inventory result is the number of garments at rest in a storage location.

Results of the Production Department for one week might be 163,000 garments. It is very easy to refer to those as results, but the inventory of the garments that are in the warehouse also can be reviewed as results entirely apart from the activity of producing them.

A natural tendency is to regard results as an activity only. Once one acquires the insight of also looking at results as an inventory, results are amplified. For example, sales of $20,000,000 during the year are the result of Sales Department activities. But, in stating that result with an inventory method of expression, there are 10,000 customers. The results, therefore, of the Sales Department are 10,000 active customers. If we aim at pushing the number up to 12,000, the dollar volume of sales will probably follow automatically. The sales are in the past; the customers are here now.

In another illustration the activity in dollars and cents for advertising would be measured, let us say, at $400,000 per year. That is a result, but it is not the result in which we are interested. The result in which we are interested is measured more in terms of the number of people who recognize our brand as the result of advertising.

Just as the activities need recording, inventories need counting.

R 2–4: *Total Units*

In totaling units, the entire amount is ascertained by adding the units together, summing up, or aggregating. This is opposite from subtracting, breaking down, or analyzing.

Executives are generally confronted with limitations to their time and sometimes find it expedient to work with totals first. Other executives, however, become immersed in the details or the units of a situation. They seldom have time to consolidate the information into one total representing the full scope. They spend so much time and effort in preparing the figures, in breaking them down and analyzing them, that they do not encourage the natural inclination to take a total view of the situation. This unit total is the complete answer in terms of figures. Executives need these totals as well as the supporting figures in their possession.

Expressing Particulars as a way of considering an executive situation illustrates among other things the importance of the total situation, the future as well as the past, in the present. At the *Reviewing Results* step, for instance, *Expression of Particulars* would be difficult if not impossible unless this consideration had been anticipated in *Expression of the Plan*. Then is the time to prepare for *Expressing Results* in terms comparable to expectations. For such forethought, relations must be analyzed.

VI

Analyzing Relations

Webster's New International Dictionary defines "Relation" as "Any aspect or quality which can be predicated only of two or more things taken together, as direction, resemblance, or of one thing considered as a factor of itself as self-identity." In EOT these relations are visualized as being aspects in which things have to do with one another considered especially from the general point of view of interest, efficiency or purpose. Relationship is a pattern of connections existing between two or more things or individuals, existing in addition to the characteristics of each separate element. It may be recognized intuitively more than it is consciously visualized or formally expressed. We are sometimes prone to emphasize the several elements connected by the relationship, rather than the less evident but significant relationship itself. The elements are usually easier to see than the connecting relation, which may be more worthy of separate consideration. These connections form the basis of the relationship, and by reason of their existence, two or more elements are visualized as being brought together. This connection becomes a "relation."

The most simple relation is a dual relation between two factors. Even the dual relation may be visualized as a complex, three-part pattern made up of the first and second elements as well as the connecting member.

As the related factors increase in number, a network or pattern of relations is formed. In business operations this pattern connects the elements in the field of relationships into an organic whole, in which any change in one element or relation is transmitted to and affects the entire network. This is borne out by the common expression that things do not get done in a vacuum. This mutual involvement pattern is made up of the relations as much as it is of the elements related. A relationship pattern thus should be visualized not as a single whole or unit but as a multiplicity. To this should also be added the factor of change which time brings on.

This pattern of relations is exemplified by organization charts which present levels of authority and groupings of functions. This device reduces relations to a more definite character. Thus, the relations between a forelady and a machine operator may be one of organization level and line of authority, and the relation of the operator to the maintenance mechanic one of functional specialization.

The "relativity" concept may furnish some clues to relations, as relations may be internal or essential and external or even non-essential. From an executive's viewpoint relativity must be considered with "particularity," as a particular situation cannot objectively exist unless the three factors of event, time, and place exist concurrently. Many of the abstractions which he draws from concrete situations, however, are relations he has projected or formulated. Relations may have tangible continuity, even when thus viewed abstractly, as they may exist in the present and in the past and may be foreseen as to the future. Posted storm warnings, for example, have a connection with our immediate welfare.

The twelve EOT emphasis areas involve basic relationships. Frequent relationships are those involving time and the relative magnitude of figures. Related certainties and satisfactions often occupy an executive's attention. The analysis and coordination of relations within an area of action involve different factors, and although the complex pattern is difficult to visualize, the relations within it have a profound bearing upon the course of management events.

The degree of firmness or fluidity (that is, the relative fixed and controllable nature) of relations is frequently considered in executive operations. The logical relation of subjects is significantly evident in topic grouping.

Certain actions may illustrate some relations; for example, executives frequently alternate between construction and criticism, between inductive and deductive approaches, and between identifying a subject by definition and example. Dual relations not involving action are those of distance and discrimination between two subjects. Ratio, relative frequency, immediacy, duration, and antecedence all may form a basis for the existence of a relation. Most of these relations involve a simple basis connecting two polar extremities.

The executive clarifies his understanding of relationships by the process of analyzing. In this process, he sets up a structure for associating elements or groupings of material for comparison, contrast, or observation. His purpose is to expose opportunities frequently not evident on the surface, but becoming self-evident upon successful analysis. Analyzing, thus, is dividing and rearranging a body of material for a logical purpose. Successful completion of an analysis implies an orderliness of relations in summary and final form.

Before the executive starts analyzing, he is concerned with the composition of the material to be analyzed; for example, the participants, the influences, or the involvements. This executive operating material, an intellectual substance, is given form by analysis. Listing the elements in simple alphabetical order dissolves preconceptions of relations.

Human relations are so close to the executive's field of awareness that he may be tempted to emphasize them to the exclusion of other relations. He may understand human relations better if he first tries to get an ordered visualization of relations in general, as an impersonal concept, before attempting to assemble content elements related to human relations. Subsequent sections of this chapter indicate guides to analysis of relationships.

ANALYZING RELATIONS: EXPOSE CONDITIONS

C 3–1: Discover Involvements

In analyzing relations, perception of the related nature of previously known facts is an early consideration. In any situation every element or factor is involved with other factors. In EOT this condition of interrelation is called "involvement." The executive needs to find these involvements and learn their relationship. He develops the full scope of relations only when he discovers this network of mutual involvement.

Involvements connect participants, influences, or factors, and are evident when one step must be completed before another can be started or if one identifiable factor causes another.

In addition to these factors involved with each other, the executive searches for those independent factors that may be handled separately. These separables are direct opposites to involvements but serve to highlight the valid involvements. If the independent factors are separated from the involved factors, they can be put into action earlier and simplify the area with which the executive is concerned. Isolating these separables is discussed later in this chapter.

A common involvement in executive relations is the contact between individuals working together. This includes group work in a conference and contacts between several individuals. Studies of contacts between Williamson-Dickie executives indicate that contacts of one person with another are the most frequent. More total time is spent in this dual relationship.

The human factor is frequently viewed as an isolated individual not vitally related to a surrounding pattern. Nevertheless, conditions require consideration of an individual's inseparable involvement with his organization.

C 3–2: Relate Factors

A factor is one of the elements or parts possessing an effective force which enables the whole facility or operation to perform a certain kind of work.

Relate means to connect or bring into relation, to show the relation of; to establish the relation between. In relating factors the executive perceives a basis of relationship of the factors. The basis of the relationship describes or gives grounds for the relationship. Such operating material as purposes, particulars, ideas, conditions, etc., are factors which can be related. Cost versus worth are significant factors to relate.

Many financial and operating reports contain factors related to one another in a single document. By relating these factors to one another, the executive can perceive critical relationships that will indicate the proper decision. In sales analysis, an executive will often attempt to relate factors in a salesman's performance that will lead to more sales productivity.

C 3–3: Project Dimensions

The executive often must visualize dimensions touching segments of operating material throughout a situation. Dimension is the quality of extent or magnitude from predetermined extreme points or positions. To project is to cast forward in order to determine these positions. Once determined, this dimension may be used to guide consideration along the line of that particular dimension.

The line between the start and the finish of an activity might be called a chronological dimension. When executives can visualize a line or sequence or dimension in a consideration area, they are in a better position to expose relationships.

Studying the work flow aids in the isolation of some of these complex relationships in a manufacturing operation. Some months ago an engineer was assigned an item called Bundle Handling Procedure. He was asked to study the flow of one bundle of garment components throughout the plant from the time it left the cutting table until it was a finished product. He followed each unit or bundle along the dimension of each stage it experienced in the process series. This study revealed that certain parts such as garment flies and facings, needed for subassembly preparation several hours ahead of the garment backs and fronts, were being cut *after* the backs and fronts. A helpful resequencing of the order of work on the various parts was developed.

After reviewing the situation in this linear sequence, it may be possible to bring in a two-dimensional cross-classification. Then, if breaks appear at certain individuals or functions in the consecutive operations in a flow, opportunities for simplifying relations may be revealed.

Bipolar dimensions are sometimes visualized. For example, balancing refinement extremes involves a dimension which calls for an optimum point between the two extremes, as does the range between consistency and effectiveness. An attempt to describe each extreme may help to clarify the relationship between them.

One type of dimension frequently used by executives is the breakdown scheme discussed under Infer Breakdown Schemes in this chapter. The breakdown scheme dimension permits visualization of the full or total scope as well as the parts represented by its elements. Operating statements estimated for six months into the future are dimensions projected at periodic intervals. If a dimension is once successfully used, it may be reapplied to similar situations. In fact, parallel comparison of two material patterns designed for the same purpose independently of each other is a very useful exposure technique. If each pattern is arranged along the lines of the same dimension, the similar areas may be included without further question. The dissimilar areas may be those indicating opportunities to investigate further.

C 3–4: Circumscribe Inclusions

The executive must cover the waterfront. He needs a generalized perspective, so as to study all operations under his individual responsibility. He needs to watch the extent and content of visualization of each item under consideration, however, so as to control the scope of inclusion. He may include so much material that the subject becomes unwieldy. On the other hand, he often exposes conditions not previously considered which are necessary for effective operations. He must then broaden his scope of inclusion or perspective to include these factors.

Elements of content material included in the executive's frame of reference become component or subordinate parts within a subject or scope. When the executive circumscribes, he draws a mental line around the subject matter included in his frame of reference, thereby excluding irrelevant or external material.

Occasionally an executive must focus his attention upon the full scope. He often finds that others in receiving his statements move to a narrower level of generality. When this occurs, he must realign the scopes of inclusion. Factors external and internal to the area may serve to help position the encircling boundary visualized, so that a mutual identification of scope can be achieved. The exclusion and inclusion of points considered frequently are used to identify the scope of a subject of consideration.

In a company acquired by purchase, our staff discovered that the definition of "current accounts receivable" used in the acquired company differed significantly from that used in the parent company. Accounts as high as $20,000.00 with invoices as much as a year old, were considered "current" by the subsidiary, because monthly extension of terms had been granted. These extensions thus made the accounts "current" within their broad definition.

Our accounting executives felt compelled to reconcile these conflicting definitions. In so doing, they wrote a new definition of "current accounts receivable" for the subsidiary's use in classifying accounts. The cooperating executives shifted scopes to the narrower frame of reference, circumscribing the definition's inclusions in the process.

ANALYZING RELATIONS: DEVELOP IDEAS

I 3–1: *Associate Similarities*

The threshold of ideas exists where two subjects are seen as being related in a way heretofore indefinitely visualized. Ideas are first visualized as abstractions, mainly because the relation between any two operating particulars is seldom concrete.

As ideas result from association, subject matter can be arranged for comparison or contrast. To associate similarities we bring together those things that resemble each other in one or more details or characteristics. Linking these resemblances frequently produces ideas.

Associating other similar instances with the problem at hand may reveal clues for a solution. This was true in August, 1957 when increased sales bogged down the already inadequate production estimating formula. The production estimate's accuracy was especially critical at that time of the year both from the standpoint of deliveries and the year-end financial position. An idea was proposed to compare the proven sales estimating formula with that of the production estimate. This comparison exposed opportunities for improving the production formula.

The executive can support his insights into an indefinite situation in the same manner. Comparing the present situation with the earlier instances often exposes concrete reasons for the insights.

Determining the subtle distinctions between similarities also may lead to opportunities to select and eliminate nonessentials.

I 3–2: *Infer Breakdown Schemes*

In assembling a number of content elements within a situation the executive will soon find that certain elements seem to come together naturally. He thus infers or induces a category, which may be used to represent a section of the full scope. When other categories are inferred he may have several elements of a breakdown scheme suitable for grouping basic segments of the entire situation. A breakdown scheme is a group of subdivisional elements of a main topic, divided at points along one logical and relevant dimension. To infer is to find out or derive by reasoning, either deductive or inductive. It is the means of classifying material into categories.

Sometimes clues to categories may be found by first looking for natural breaks or groupings in a sequence and then developing a title representing each span or section of the series. This leads to a break-down scheme of the entire series, using categories of a more general level than the average original entry of the series. This method calls primarily for an inductive approach. Sometimes, too, after content elements have been listed and before they are grouped into breakdown scheme categories, an intermediate step of sequencing these elements can be carried out. This sequencing, although requiring extra time, frequently leads into a more valid breakdown scheme.

A convenient number of elements in a breakdown scheme is six. Two and four elements are simplest: six provides a finer breakdown; more than ten elements may be too numerous to be easily dealt with. Industrial engineers frequently break down cycle times of a production operation, even though the entire operation for one piece may not take over .33 minutes.

Executives frequently use breakdown schemes in analysis for the purpose of formulating ideas. An example of a breakdown scheme which itself is designed to suggest ideas is, as follows:

Why is it necessary?
What purpose does it have?
Where is the best place to do it?
When is the best time to do it?
Who should do it?
How should it be done?

A breakdown scheme may be used in the Accounting Department and in a different application in the Production Department. Terminology and breakdown schemes of company reports should be standardized to facilitate reference and comparison. After noting the universality of breakdown schemes, executives may begin collecting schemes frequently used in their company. These may become useful, particularly after they are indexed for reference. The schemes which are illustrated here are only a few of the collection of sixty or more which Williamson-Dickie executives have selected to illustrate schemes used in their operations.

Many incomplete breakdown schemes exist in an organization which would be much more useful if they were completed. A breakdown scheme of personnel factors is not as useful when only the first five factors are given; for example,

1. Employment
2. Training
3. Placement

4. Compensation
5. Performance Measurement

as when the pattern is filled out with:

6. Working Conditions
7. Welfare

Existing breakdown schemes may be studied for clues to fill out incomplete patterns of schemes inductively developed. Discussions and consultations with others frequently help fill out this incomplete pattern. Patterns as relations are practically infinite, and a large part of that stock of memory of past activities which executives call experiences may consist largely of abstract patterns with which they have some familiarity. This familiarity may be intuitive, or it may be more definite in nature.

There are two types of breakdown schemes—tangible and abstract. Tangible breakdown schemes are more easily understood because executives come in conscious contact with them frequently. They are induced from tangible, physical operating problems or material. They have no gradation of scope, extent or intensity, as would be the case in a reduction scheme. The Personnel Factors breakdown scheme listed above has an abstract base which may be useful to people unfamiliar with the terminology of the clothing industry.

The use of a breakdown scheme is illustrated by the evolution of the Dickie Dealer Profit Plan. At the close of World War II, Williamson-Dickie faced the fact that it sold a large proportion of its business to chain stores under their private labels. Disadvantages of this arrangement too numerous to list here led to the decision to concentrate all efforts upon promoting the "Dickie" brand. This also meant that new customers must be found who would carry "Dickies" garments. The decision created many new items on which to get results. The story of these combined efforts was summarized in *Sales Management* in May, 1952.

Back of the story of Dickie Dealer Profit Plan was years of experimentation with schemes to break down the question: *What kind of relationship can we establish with our dealers which will demonstrate the profit of aggressively selling our Dickies garments?* The *Sales Management* article passes lightly over this foundation with the sentence, "The mass of material was then screened down to ten salient points, and then Dickie Dealer Profit Plan (DDPP) was built around them."

Dickie Dealer Profit Plan Elements

1. Regular Reordering Schedule
2. Competitive Pricing
3. Branded Merchandise
4. Proper Selling Display
5. Location
6. Fixtures
7. Lighting
8. Personnel
9. Planned Advertising Schedule
10. Planned Window Schedule

The 10-element breakdown scheme of DDPP elements was induced from material of a tangible operating nature. The kind of relationship with accounts which Williamson-Dickie wanted was determined inductively by research. First analyzed were particular dealers who were successful and then a group of dealers who were unsuccessful. Then the ten elements of the DDPP breakdown scheme were determined. These were the dimensions along which the mutually profitable dealer activities could be measured.

"Screening down a mass of material" is the process of inferring breakdown and reduction schemes. These schemes are the outgrowth of trial and error that never can be imagined from seeing the finished product. The reduction of subjects to a narrower scope more suitable for handling implies that the narrower element is a part of the whole subject. The part-to-whole relationship is involved frequently in executive operations. This process is discussed further at I 6–1, Simplify by Reduction.

I 3–3: Isolate Separables

One of the concerns of an executive is to avoid undue involvement of the current undertaken item. For that reason he frequently isolates or sets apart certain parts of the entire situation which are susceptible to such isolation. These separables are segments of material which, by their lack of involvement with the other material, can separate or remain independent from the other material. They are in some respects self-sufficient. When he isolates separables, he removes or separates them from other contiguous material. This effective isolation of separables is one of the products of careful analysis.

His analysis will isolate some factors the executive previously considered essential or inseparably involved in the undertaking. Action on these factors now can be delayed or even abandoned without retarding advancement of the item.

When an operating step is delaying an entire program, the executive can ask questions such as these: "Is this step vital to the entire project? Can that part be delayed?" Affirmative answers may reveal the separable nature of the step.

In the fall of 1953 conditions were quite competitive in the garment industry and it became necessary to lower garment prices. A number of cost-cutting changes were proposed and proven satisfactory. A 1¾-inch waistband could produce a savings of cloth and in addition was more acceptable to the consumer than the former 2-inch waistband. Five other cost-reducing alternatives of a similar nature were developed. Everyone had assumed that all six alternatives would be installed at the same time, but there would be several months' delay in getting the machine parts to change over from the 2-inch to the 1¾-inch waistbands. Suddenly it dawned on someone that the subjectively held involvement of all six improvements was an illusion and that the other changes could be put into effect immediately with their savings. The waistband improvement which was separable could be installed when machinery arrived.

Isolation is not merely subjectively held in an individual's mind. The isolation must actually exist. This means that when action is started, the events which actually transpire will be isolated just as they were visualized at the start. One of the defects in executive operations occurs when assumed isolations are not valid. An example of attempting to isolate inseparables occurred when the Williamson-Dickie Truck Department attempted to select and hire truck drivers without coordination with the Personnel Division. They hired men based on experience only, without considering such basic qualifications as mental alertness, cooperative record in the past, personal and moral habits, and so forth. As a result of this improper selection, dissension in the group and a serious labor situation developed.

The executive may find that the involvement of the undertaking has become so widespread and complex that further advancement is difficult or impossible. In this case the executive must move back his emphasis area to find a way to separate and isolate sections of the situation, thus permitting operation on a simpler scale than first attempted. For example, items being carried forward have a way of acquiring additional details, thus expanding the number of operating elements to consider.

For this reason it may soon become necessary to break away certain sections of the item and to continue advancing them without having frequent overall coordination meetings. It usually is desirable to get these separate sections of the item out of the way as early as possible in the advancement of the item. In fact, some sections of the original item may grow enough to become separate but coordinated items.

I 3–4: Cross-Fertilize Contributions

Too close a control over the authorship of ideas is frequently a retarding influence. Ideas are usually developed faster and with more certainty through group cooperation. The initiation and contribution of ideas by juniors, colleagues, and seniors, should be encouraged. In developing teamwork, the executive should encourage recommendations, since recommendations often furnish the material for cross-fertilization.

Contributions are alternatives offered by individuals which are useful in advancing an undertaking. Instead of considering these contributions as hindrances or distractions to be discarded, the executive receiving them seeks to develop them further. Thus cross-fertilization occurs when he favorably receives offered alternatives and uses them as clues to further advancement.

Williamson-Dickie executives have long recognized the importance of cross-fertilizing ideas. This concept has been useful in their consultant contacts and in opinion research development. Ideas from the consultant's perspective are more fruitful when cross-fertilized with those of company executives. The ideas which emerge from this cross-fertilization usually are improvements over the original contributions. Seasonal lines evolve from opinion research, which cross-fertilizes ideas from customers, salesmen, the product development department and others.

One technique in developing ideas is the use of alternation. It is much easier to criticize than to construct. In the alternating technique one person constructs and contributes a proposal. Someone else reviews and criticizes it after construction is completed. When this is done, further refinements are frequently evident. Following the criticism period, the proposal may be reconstructed with ideas developed in the discussion and again criticized. This alternation helps to impersonalize attitudes toward the material with which executives work.

Ideas seem to be a product of an atmosphere or environment which is conducive to their creation. Steps which seem to foster creativity in an executive group are: encouragement of minority opinions, allowing people to make suggestions and to experience doubtful success without being put on the defensive, and spreading knowledge of company purposes and strategies.

ANALYZING RELATIONS: UNIFY VIEWS

V 3–1: Balance Dominances

Dominance is an individual's control or influence over a situation or other individuals. Executive dominance ranges from domineering, "high-pressure" individuals to meek, Casper Milquetoast or doormat types. Executives must seek an effective balance between these two extremes. To balance is to find an optimum point between two extremes and thus establish the most suitable disposition of the factors involved without undue sacrifice of equilibrium within the total situation. Synonyms are to equalize, to center between, or to compensate.

Balancing of dominances may be practiced in an organization through the technique of assignment. It is constantly exercised in the working for, working with, and the complexities of managing authority and responsibility. People sometimes become resistant to overdominance. On the other hand, overcasualness or indifference with regard to one's own proposal may lose the interest of others.

A study of the ratio of participation by individuals in interviews will often indicate overparticipation or dominance by certain executives along with inadequate participation by others. The dominant individual's statements usually carry the gist of these interviews.

Balancing dominance and participation sometimes leads into emphasizing sentimentality at the expense of results. So-called human relations often are overemphasized to the extent that an ordinary day-to-day problem is looked upon as a "pathological" situation. Executives should endeavor to maintain a continuing high plateau of good working relationships that does not have to be rebuilt with every new conference or discussion. This permits concentration upon the job to be done rather than upon the personalities involved.

Relations between executives range from formal to informal. The junior-senior relationship is largely formal, but a senior's right to maintain dominance must be earned to be fully effective. The basis of authority often rests in the situation, but generally the senior executive is more likely to be the dominant one.

Maintaining the best balance between getting the current situation under control and developing the junior executive's skill is a recurring problem. The junior's skill may be developed to the point where he can set up an item and push it through to a conclusion in line with company strategy. The senior executive may choose to carry the ball on an item, or he may decide to coach the junior to become a more skilled executive, a somewhat less immediately rewarding approach. In the latter case, the senior calls the junior's attention to the situation, but leaves the development of the item to the junior. Specialists can offer some useful clues to the nondirective interviewing approach. In a well-conducted nondirective interview, the interviewer does not register approval, disapproval, shock or other personal reactions.

During the senior's emphasis upon nondominance the junior may include much useless material, make an incomplete investigation or fail in some other manner. On the other hand, he possibly may bring conditions to light and develop ideas which would have been overlooked by a senior executive. The overdominant executive is frequently too preoccupied with the sound of his own voice to note helpful conditions or ideas.

At one extreme in the balance of participation between senior and junior executives is the case where the senior executive is required by an unbalanced personal involvement condition to take the initiative to identify and expose all conditions, express and formulate all ideas, attempt to align views with the junior executive and to take the lead in laying out a plan of action. He also must assign the next step and then review actions step by step. At this extreme the senior executive, no doubt, is carrying more than his share of the joint responsibility for the item.

When the situation has been turned over to a junior executive, the senior executive's role in a large measure is that of a spotlight to help illuminate the situation for the junior executive. As the junior sees the necessity for action more clearly, he is in a better position to set up his own item. He thus gains the experience of carving a results-producing item out of a situation. This analogy of illumination may be applied at each step along the path outlined by the six considerations and the six steps in the EOT advancement cycle.

It is well to bear in mind that the relationship between the junior and senior executives is fundamental in working with and advancing the item, and both junior and senior should endeavor to understand the possibilities and limitations of their particular roles. Again, the important point is the emphasis on the situation and the advancement of the item it has prompted.

This discussion has treated executive dominance as an aid to advancing the item or company goal. Occasionally, however, individuals abuse their authority by overdominance and personal aggressiveness. Their influence is channeled toward advancing personal rather than company objectives. Because these executives also tend to "play favorites," cliques sometimes develop. A company-oriented executive treats individuals of coordinate rank equally without regard to his personal feelings.

V 3–2: *Communicate Information*

Exposing information renders the situation accessible to the consideration of others, transforming its status from the unknown to the known. To make the status of the situation known to others, the executive must communicate relevant information. To communicate is essentially to transmit, convey, or inform.

This communication of information usually is carried out through personal visits, contacts, conferences, letters, memorandums, and telephone calls. It can be visualized as traveling in one direction at a time and moving from the individual who initiates it to the person who receives it, although direction of communication obviously alternates within a single conference.

Exposure and prompt communication of information provides an organization with a vitalizing substance. This transmission is similar to the flow of blood through the circulatory system of the human body. If the communicating channels are not kept open, the executive organization or "body" becomes anemic. It does not function properly, since the lifegiving substance cannot flow to the terminal arteries and return to the headquarters through the communicating channels or "veins."

Personnel conditions influence the communication of information about a situation. Each executive's vitality, tenacity, and mature awareness of the operating usefulness of relevant information encourages adequate communication. Harmonious relations between members of a group and their attitudes toward communication are even more important. The environment under which information is to be disclosed greatly influences the activity.

Business conferences are effective means of communicating information, particularly when personal contributions are encouraged. If an organization is free and open in its communications, helpful operating information is more easily exposed and communicated to others.

Recorded information provides a permanent record. This information should be easily read, and the form of presentation may also be profitably emphasized. It should not be a vehicle of subjective expression, which the recipient must reorganize. Typing, distributing, duplicating, and publishing all amplify communication.

Decisions should be communicated in advance of action. When this is done, it is difficult for anyone to exceed authority without its being known by those involved. Poor communication hinders unification and causes duplicated efforts, while adequate communication in business organizations fosters harmonious, effective relations.

Occasionally information is only partially communicated, altered, or withheld entirely. The motive in these cases may be to deceive intentionally. More frequently, however, individuals are either careless or fail to recognize the consequences. Reluctance to expose facts to the view of others—especially when there is a personal involvement—sometimes causes the failure to communicate. An objective attitude and persistence until all facts are communicated expedites all executive operations.

Failure to communicate information is not confined to junior executives. Senior executives sometimes make decisions affecting a junior executive's function without notifying him. Communication between them is a two-way street, and to be effective, both lanes must be kept open.

V 3–3: *Combine Inclinations*

Inclinations are individual opinions reached by individuals either before or after investigation and deliberation. Executives in the operating group need to unite these inclinations. If one executive feels that a situation is a crisis while another feels it deserves a low priority, effective teamwork is not likely to result.

The purpose of combining inclinations is to secure an official conclusion without disregarding the free choice or personal inclinations of different individuals. At this stage the problem is to resolve these individual inclinations, so they will reappear as one without sacrificing any of the original objectives. A resolution may be found to absorb some of the conflicting views, but it may be necessary to defer some proposals until a more suitable time.

Discussion and communication of overall company strategy to the executive group usually stimulates combining inclinations. This also tends to lower the "boiling point," or the level of results at which executives are satisfied.

Each member of the group should report his minority views, and the senior executive must consider them, reconciling them into the solution if he sees fit. All share the responsibility to advance the item in spite of the few remaining unreconciled views. This is often a severe test of an individual's ability to give and take. Sometimes one must retreat with good grace from a valid position.

Generally, executive viewpoints are in alignment with company goals. On occasions, however, they do digress. When this happens, the co-ordinating executive must bring conflicting views into alignment with the firm's objectives. Such a move is important, as individuals with conflicting views can seriously retard item advancement.

The individual with conflicting views also can influence others un-favorably. A supervisor at Williamson-Dickie's main warehouse opposed the installation of a wage incentive program for warehouse personnel, even though incentive rates had been proved satisfactory in similar operations. His views on the subject influenced a newly appointed Division Sales Manager to oppose the project. As the Division Sales Manager was in charge of the warehouse, advancement on the item stopped until the problem spot could be located. When the DSM's views were aligned, the incentive program was allowed to proceed on its own merits.

The inclinations of individuals whose personal desires conflict with company objectives cannot be effectively combined with others. These individuals are inclined to oppose or modify assignments. They fre-quently become evasive when attempts are made to combine inclinations. This undesirable characteristic is discussed in greater detail at V 1–2: Share Interests.

At this step the executive group should exercise care that no pertinent views are excluded. In 1959, Williamson-Dickie was experimenting with resin finishes to improve wash-and-wear characteristics of twills. At that time an experimental sample had been produced. Certain manufacturing executives called a meeting to discuss its suitability with the General Manager and Research Director. The General Manager noted, however, that the Quality Control Manager, whose viewpoint was an essential consideration at this stage of the project, had not been included in the discussion.

V 3–4: *Mediate Group Opinions*

It is usually necessary to unify the views of individuals in order to get an item or a next step started into action. For this reason the executive must mediate group opinions on actions yet to be taken. His role is a kind of mediating or balancing operation which distributes and integrates the diverse values held by individuals toward a common purpose of the organization.

The executive may not be able to achieve harmony of group opinion immediately. The proposed alternative frequently is not acceptable to all concerned. In this case he may ask for suggestions from those concerned. An unrestrained exchange of alternatives in such a discussion often will uncover an alternate solution on which all can agree.

At Williamson-Dickie the method of collecting past due accounts from salesmen had been a source of disagreement. The accounting manager felt that these accounts should be collected immediately. The Sales Manager, on the other hand, felt that forcing the issue would create friction with the salesmen. The salesmen had never been pressed to pay charges for their samples, and some of them owed several hundred dollars. All agreed, however, that the sizable sum involved should be paid. One executive suggested sending invoices at the same time a planned general salary increase was mailed. This alternative might satisfy both departments involved. Timing was an important consideration here, as it is in similar situations.

The coordinating executive should follow a discussion carefully, as conflicts may arise from incompatible factors. He should search aggressively for alternatives which will avoid an impasse. Voting is frequently useful in dealing with a number of individual views. Voting may reveal the nature and extent of an unsuspected minority. The criticism and comments of the group probably will improve the ideas as well as the emerging plan. Voting elicits opinions from the silent members who follow the practice of not speaking unless their opinion is asked.

Generally, participating executives should search for a third solution that may satisfy a more substantial proportion of the group. On the other hand, the mediating executive may not judge it practicable to prolong the discussion to a unanimous decision. Since advancement frequently stops because of overrefinement, the leader may assist the group to arrive at a working estimate in such cases. He should be especially alert to opportunities for harmonious group decisions. These are matters to be judged by the leader or mediating individual.

Each member of the group should adjust to the consensus of an intelligent majority of the group. If the members are qualified people and have put on record their sincerely considered opinions, any one individual should consider carefully before opposing this consensus.

If each individual has followed the proceedings closely, he should not be surprised by the majority consensus. Usually he should endeavor to adjust to these group opinions. He may need to change his views to fit the external situation without disturbing his sense of satisfaction. A maturing executive needs to learn that he gains stature and respect when he readily reverses his position, if it is indicated by objective facts or capable opinions. If these precautions are followed, the executive usually secures the approval and support of the group.

Junior members of the group should realize that mediation by leaders is frequently imperfect. To get results, the organization needs perfect seniors no more than perfect juniors.

ANALYZING RELATIONS: DETERMINE PLANS

P 3–1: Integrate Compatible Factors

Compatible factors are those factors in a situation suitable to the accomplishment of a purpose which because of their nature and qualities are capable of co-existing in harmony. For effective operations, the various factors involved within a situation need to be integrated.

Frequently material has been assembled in different locations, where it has been worked on at different times, without tie-ins with the previous efforts. Integration takes place when all compatible factors are combined at one principal location. This integration is the merging or combining of factors into a class, group, or category for a harmonious and functional relationship. The unit or whole desired is a cohesive, logically structured system. Factors in a situation are compatible or belong together because of their functional, geographical, or logical relationship. Failing to integrate them may bring about an artificial or apparently illogical plan.

Irrelevant or separable factors must be recognized. When such material is excluded, integrating the factors into one entire pattern will require less effort.

After factors are integrated, will they stay integrated? They are likely to if their structure is sound and logical. Frequently, however, there are competing patterns and scopes of inclusion. Breakdown schemes and the sequence of their elements can expose clues to such disintegrating influences. New facts and considerations frequently appear when plans are put into action which also may alter a previously integrated pattern. Individuals as well as material factors must be integrated for coordinated effort. Building a team spirit or feeling of belonging is an important aspect of such integration. This team spirit is illustrated by the football coach who built up the "Suicide Seven" team of linemen. Sometimes the sharing of a common desire or aim—or, on the other hand, a common misfortune—will bring individuals together.

An orchestra leader on a recent television show illustrated integration of factors. A sizable orchestra and supporting cast was involved. The leader, nevertheless, continued the theme melody and general spirit of the show in such a way that individual instrumentation and individual background could be recognized. He permitted each musician to keep the spotlight for a short period with a series of renditions, while the whole program remained well coordinated. As in an orchestra, the goal in an organization, although difficult to achieve, is to have each factor join and support advancement rather than interfere with it. Such achievement is a reward in itself.

P 3–2: Lay Out Cross-Classifications

Earlier in this chapter the part played by one breakdown scheme is stressed. The material within a situation may be susceptible to subdivision by more than one breakdown scheme. To lay out two breakdown schemes to cross-analyze such material presents a two-dimensional picture of the situation, a cross-classification. To *lay out* is to plan, design, or display an arrangement.

These *cross-classifications* are two-dimensional arrangements for interrelating informational content. In a cross-classification the elements of one breakdown scheme head vertical columns from left to right, and the other breakdown scheme is distributed from top to bottom and is represented by horizontal lines. This arrangement is frequently called a cross- or tabular-analysis. It is frequently used by executives to relate material in a convenient form. They are utilized to simplify the arrangement of material too complex to handle easily. Material laid out in cross-tabular form is easily referred to and facilitates logical grouping and comparison. Such a presentation also simplifies evaluation and selection, especially when numerous elements are involved.

Skill is needed in handling these schemes, especially in matching concrete particulars to abstract generalities and in arranging the assembled content elements into an ordered cross-classification.

Annual sales, for example, can be broken down by first, second, third, and fourth quarters of the year along a dimension of time; and again broken down geographically by sales divisions of north, south, east, and west. This cross-classification contains sixteen categories within which to distribute the results. Each of the four lines and four columns can be totaled for further information.

The EOT Chart, some expense budgets, and organization charts also are arranged in a cross-tabular manner. In organizing two breakdown schemes for cross-classification, it is necessary that each breakdown scheme have universal application. The EOT Chart now consists of a cross-classification of six steps and six considerations. This permits identification of executive responses and material within an executive situation according to any one of the 36 such cross-related categories. This more precise level of refinement satisfies identification requirements within the EOT Pattern.

One undertaking which permitted cross-classification of operating information was Williamson-Dickie branch factory expense. In this case the breakdown scheme by locations of eight factories was universally applicable. There was, however, no universally applicable breakdown scheme for types of personnel. Various methods of classifying personnel were examined by which to distribute payroll expense uniformly. The most satisfactory was a Personnel Department breakdown used as a basis for vacations, bonuses, and other fringe benefits. It classified personnel starting with salaried supervision, then proceeding to salaried staff, hourly supervision, hourly staff, and so on. This breakdown scheme universal to all branch plants was utilized. This cross-classification permitted weekly and monthly reports showing the expenses of individual branch plants and also the total payroll expense for each personnel classification.

P 3–3: Organize Functions

Much literature and discussion by management experts has been devoted to functional organization. Attempting to cover a subject already so professionally developed would be useless repetition here. The operation of a functional organization cannot be visualized from books alone. Organization specialists are available for consultation with executives on this subject.

As Williamson-Dickie executives visualize it, a *function* is an activity or operation expected of an executive unit by virtue of its status or position. This activity accomplishes the usefulness, end, or purpose of the particular position. It is the work expected to be performed or the activity appropriate to that position.

Much executive effort is spent in organizing material, functions, and individuals to work together as a unit. When the executive *organizes*, he arranges, systematizes, or gets into working order.

Organizing functions or human activity is more subtle and complex than organizing operating material. In organizing functions, the executive ties undertakings into the organization. He groups like duties together and attempts to minimize the number of responsibility centers. In this effort, he will distinguish between line and staff functions. This activity does not include adapting the organization to the individual, which some executives frequently attempt.

An important way to clarify and communicate functional responsibility is to have the group members who are to carry out particular items explore and discuss various phases of the situation. Ideally, if this exposure of the situation has been complete, each executive should take the initiative in carving out parts of the item for which he is functionally responsible.

A senior executive may undertake a complex item that needs to be divided into parts. These parts should if possible be sufficiently isolated to make them independent items that will require little detailed coordination by the senior executive. Such an item was the establishing of a new Williamson-Dickie branch factory. Because this subject covered almost every function of the enterprise, it was very shortly divided into three major functions: facilities, personnel, and reports and records. In this way the *plant and facilities* item could be assigned to the Factory Manager, the *personnel and organization development* item could be assigned to the Personnel Director, and the *reports and records* item could be taken over by the Treasurer. These three sections, although they were related, would not require rigid coordination. For this reason they were suitable for isolation as separate items to be handled by these different executives.

Organization charts graphically illustrate the functions, responsibility levels, and structure of the organic whole of the operating organization. Executive action on undertaken items flows through the functional channels which such charts illustrate.

Undertaken items relating to the organization of human effort are susceptible to the same operating techniques as any item. Conditions are first exposed; the organizational channels being followed by individuals in their ordinary communications are then compared with the organization chart. This concept of the organization of human effort is discussed in this guide point, although functional organization is separate from individual responsibility in the organization structure, discussed next under the heading Assign Accountabilities.

The problem of changes in an organization differs from the problem of decisions within the framework of the existing organization. The former involves major rearrangements of human relationships.

P 3–4: Assign Accountabilities

An *accountability* is the delegated custody and responsibility for an undertaking or function placed with an individual whose duty is to report upon its performance. The fulfillment of an obligation, the execution of a trust, and the administration of an office are within the limits of the responsible person's power and obligation. To *assign* is to deliberately delegate responsibility for an undertaking to an individual, to hand over, or to charge him with the shouldering of this obligation. Functions, broad continuing objectives, items, and next steps are examples of accountabilities of varying scope which can be assigned to executives.

"Who should do it?" is usually the first question asked when it is necessary to assign accountability. Organizational channeling, personnel, individual responsibility, and jurisdiction are all involved. Common sense should be exercised with regard to the senior executive's retaining certain items and delegating other types of items. Development items, such as ones pertaining to establishing a new plant, are more likely to be personally participated in by top management than items such as the setting up of another assembly line in the factory.

Effective assigning of accountabilities entails more than merely designating an individual to accept a certain responsibility. The assigning executive should fully expect the responsible individual to accept this accountability. This expectancy should be based on the accountable individual's reliability and probable ability to carry out the assignment. The attempted assigning of accountability may build a bridge over one-half of a span; the acceptance of accountability completes the bridge of action.

It is desirable that the executive who has been assigned accountability for a next step feel responsibility for the item as a whole and not for that next step only. For an executive to shoulder his responsibility consistently, he must be able at the outset to visualize the central issue of the item through to its end. Lack of vision denies some executives an understanding of the possibilities of useful situations. Here is where the senior executive may make a direct contribution by discussing the situation with the executive who is to work with the item. He may point out how this situation is blocking the progress of the company as a whole. He may point out the many functions that are related to the situation. When the executives who are responsible for these different functions participate in a conference, this multiplies the senior executive's contribution.

When the executive makes assignments, he should know the structural nature of the organization. He can weaken accountability for assignments if he bypasses individuals with previously assigned accountabilities or fails to follow the proper organization channels in assignments and communication. The organization structure itself should have no conflicting rules and jurisdiction so that the group may function harmoniously.

One of the accountabilities of an executive is to coordinate the efforts of the several individuals reporting directly to him. The individuals in this group should share with him the responsibility for their own team's effectiveness. To accomplish this the executive sometimes makes "coordinate assignments," which are simultaneous assignments given to two or more individuals who are to work together for a common result.

Coordinate assignments are more effective when they originate spontaneously. A case in which coordinate responsibility functioned forcefully took place when members of the Texas Manufacturers Association prevailed upon a Williamson-Dickie executive to accept the chairmanship of its local chapter. He accepted this responsibility unwillingly because of the pressure of other duties. The active members of the chapter willingly cooperated, however, and their joint efforts in making plans for the chapter were noticeably effective.

Group participation in planning helps to produce sound accountability. Plans should be understood by those who carry them into action; thus the educational value of participating in planning has a multiple usefulness to those who produce results.

ANALYZING RELATIONS: PRODUCE ACTIONS

A 3–1: Utilize Availables

Much of the executive's effort up to this time has been spent on steps which are preliminaries to action. He should now be ready to produce action. He must, if at all possible, resist the impulse for further preparation and work with what he has—in other words, utilize available resources.

Available resources are facilities which can immediately and conveniently be relied upon as an aid to action. They are the expedients or the instrumentalities that the executive may presently utilize. At this stage, the executive should make full and profitable use of any of these available facilities.

He may face the tendency to back up and spend more time getting things in shape to take action. If he is not careful, he may start a new and bigger project or more nonproductive preparation for action. The going may not be smooth, as his plans may not be as refined as he had originally intended. Preliminaries may not be as completely prepared, and facilities may not be arranged. At this critical juncture, he needs to decide whether to stop action and start over again or to utilize what is now available and proceed with action. He must evaluate the need to push action. An example would be to compare the cost of proceeding with inadequate facilities versus the cost of a delay for adequate preparation.

The executive should not plan on utilizing something that is not available. In this respect, the relationship between controllable and fixed conditions is similar to that between available and unavailable facilities.

The executive's enthusiasm and resourcefulness are important in keeping the item advancing toward a conclusion. Often a workable status when properly utilized is sufficient for action.

A 3–2: Adapt to Developments

Change in circumstances is an inevitable factor in executive operations. The executive must accept the fact that he is "shooting at a moving target." He may find it easier to look at the situation at rest on a printed or written page; but in doing this he is seeing the situation as it existed at only one instant in its motion and advancement. The situation is changing, with new developments constantly appearing. Whether these developments come about by accident or by design is of little consequence in recognizing the fact that situations *do* change.

Developments might be defined as recently revealed conditions, frequently unforeseen or not provided for, which significantly affect the advancement of an undertaken item. They are the circumstances and the evolving contingencies which grow out of objective action. They are the realities to which the executive must adapt.

The executive must adjust or accommodate to developments in a situation. He may find, for example, that developments put a new light on the end-result originally desired, and he may find it wise to abandon the item entirely. For this reason it is desirable to foresee and prevent excessive deviation from the agreed next step. Further, in designing a plan, one should provide for additional involvements. This is done in designing a report form by providing space in the form for entering revisions, deletions, and substitutions. These provisions for mobility and flexibility for item changes aid the executive in adapting to developments. No plan is rigidly predetermined in every detail before action.

The item "Press Room Ventilation" reveals the experience of some Williamson-Dickie executives in adapting to developments. This item was set up because operators had complained that the press room air conditioning was inadequate. During interviews with individual operators concerning conditions in the press room, it became clear that the scope of the situation was much larger than cooling alone, as operators also complained of fatigue and inability to meet their production standards. An air-conditioning engineer made recommendations to improve cooling for the press room operators, and action was produced by installing an extra washed-air unit. In adapting to developments covering the entire situation, further action was also produced by installing new press machines with automatic closing devices which gave the operators more productive time with less strain.

A 3–3: Overcome Obstacles

Inherent in almost every situation that reaches the executive's attention are obstacles to producing action. These are conditions or developments which, if not resolved or overcome, may stop item advancement. They are the difficulties, obstructions, and hindrances that must be overcome. These interferences or restrictions to item advancement may be external conditions, or they may be individuals with negative or difficult personalities. He must meet and dispose of them, clear them out of the way, remove them, or work around them.

Overcoming obstacles is a major executive function, and the executive should orient himself to and expect them. He should be prepared for obstacles of one kind or another, and he should attack them with an aggressive, hopeful attitude. He should not borrow trouble by assuming that ordinary obstacles are impossibilities. Instead, he should start cutting through "red tape."

An obstacle should not be looked upon as insurmountable or as a frustrating block to advancement; but as a challenge to overcome so that advancement can proceed. Occasionally, the executive's resourcefulness may even turn obstacles into advantages or conveniences. In any event, the executive must find a way to lessen the delaying effect of impediments in order to reach the objective without unreasonably modifying it. Overcoming an obstacle may require every executive operating technique available as long as it remains in the path of the item. Frequently the executive is unsuccessful in working around an obstacle because he has skipped an essential step and is not on the logical next step.

Immature executives sometimes feel that an obstacle should be surmounted on the first attempt. Experience does not bear this out. It would be foolish to think that a football player expects a touchdown every time he carries the ball. Just as in football, the executive must make many separate advancement efforts to make headway in a difficult situation. If he cannot get results on an item by starting at one place, he should start again at another. Looking back upon completed items, the executive will usually find that some items he expected to complete within a few weeks actually took several months to produce permanent improvement.

A 3–4: *Consult Advisers*

An *adviser* is a qualified individual who can contribute approaches, techniques, and points of view, but who is not necessarily expected to assume responsibility for putting his advice into effect. Advisers are counsellors, consultants, or authorities. *Consulting advisers* in EOT means calling upon another individual who by experience, skill, or knowledge is in a position to contribute information useful in handling a situation. An executive can extend his abilities substantially by making full use of advisers. By seeking advice and conferring with these advisers, he extends his own perspectives considerably.

An executive should not necessarily consult advisers at the first appearance of trouble. If he has extended every effort to keep the item advancing and has failed to overcome obstacles, he should then recognize that advisers' counsel might be helpful. Sometimes an executive feels that because he has not been able to contribute to the advancement of a problem, it cannot be advanced at all. He should realize that while advice and consultation from others may not necessarily solve the problem, it frequently will yield an alternative which he himself can cross-fertilize into a solution. Advice from consultants, in viewing the situation from another perspective, helps the executive determine if his present activities are aimed at the desired target. It may be that the next step assigned is, in its present interpretation, unreasonable or impossible.

Executives are encouraged, therefore, to seek assistance for their own efforts and abilities in advancing undertaken items. It is a good practice to retain sound counsel and to seek advice from respected authorities. Associates in the organization are generally ready and willing to help their colleagues, juniors, and seniors.

Independent consultants outside the organization who are experts in their particular fields can also be called upon for advice. With a perspective quite different from that of permanent company executives, their advice often yields clues to overcome obstacles which may seem insurmountable to the company executive. Cross-fertilization of this advice with company executives' proposals is usually even more effective.

A consultant who is retained too long may exhaust his contributions. The more highly specialized consultants "run out of soap" more quickly than their counterparts in more general fields. Executives should also recognize that consultants are not necessarily qualified to advise on matters outside of their particular field. A consultant specializing in garment methods may save a good deal of money for the firm in that area. He probably is not qualified to reorganize the manufacturing organization, even though he may suggest such a move.

ANALYZING RELATIONS: REVIEW RESULTS

R 3–1: *Align Comparables*

Executives must cultivate the habit of checking to determine if factors to be compared are truly comparable. These factors, which Williamson-Dickie executives have termed "Comparables," are two or more representative segments of material of the same category. The scope, breakdown, and sequence arrangement of each comparable unit should align sufficiently to permit comparison or contrast with another. To align is to make similar two or more separate pieces of information so they can be considered in relation or in opposition to each other; that is, to correlate, correspond, or parallel. The figures in the units compared may be different, but the comparable unit itself needs to be aligned. Aligning comparables is essential when planned and actual results are compared. Uniformity of titles and arrangement of the recorded material lessens the organizing required at this point.

Making unlike units comparable is a time-consuming but necessary job. Executives are almost continuously called upon to bring information pertaining to operations, methods, and results into a comparable state. For example, planned sales expressed in numbers of garments and actual sales expressed in dollars are not comparable and must be translated into the same type of unit. Another example of noncomparable information would be the use of a quarter-year of three calendar months on one report and a quarter with two four-week and one five-week period on another. The novice sometimes endeavors to compare gross production figures with net production figures from which rejects have been deducted. Executives must develop the awareness that such information is not comparable until it is brought into alignment.

The results of the item at the time of completion are peculiar to it. In this way results have a cut-off point. All planned results of an item should, if possible, have the same period ending. This is sometimes not feasible, however. It may be necessary, for example, to have one cut-off point for counting production and another one for payroll cost calculation. In such a case, provision for aligning of comparables should be included in the design of control records. The executive should keep in mind, however, the difficulty of comparing production inventory figured to one cut-off point by the Accounting Department (e.g., July 28) with figures calculated to another cut-off point by the Manufacturing Department (e.g., July 31).

In addition to the simple, dual relation of comparing one element with another, executives frequently find it effective to compare one series of elements with another series. In production, the comparison of an operator's job description with the actual working method would be an example. Comparison of identical, similar, and different methods of results is of the same category.

Comparing two different sets of similar information is "parallel comparison." This technique is useful in integrating reports of similar information by different divisions of the company. For example, if two independent groups or individual efforts have dealt with the same situation or material, then each group's report would have individual characteristics as to breakdown scheme, sequence, inclusions, numbers, or symbols. When these reports are brought together, however, parallel comparison is impossible unless comparables have been aligned.

A complete parallel comparison is also useful in exposing opportunities and omissions, as it almost automatically forces an objective consideration of a situation.

R 3–2: Compare Entries

After comparables are aligned, the executive compares the entries. An *entry* is a statement or set of figures written down on paper. It also may be called recorded material, notations, or records. Unrecorded details, oral reports, or omissions, of course, are not entries.

Comparing includes finding out how and to what degree things are similar or different, and expressing the difference. "Check conformities" and "collate" are synonymous, while "contrast" is a closely related operation and may be considered at the same time.

The comparison of entries may be carried out at various scope levels— at the full scope, between elements of breakdown schemes, between different periods of time, and between planned results and results accumulated to date.

Comparing results with estimates and determining the deviations of operating performance also call for comparison of entries. One comparison frequently made in executive operations is between one activity in a series or flow, and the preceding or following activity.

Making a parallel comparison between two different groups of similar operating material, organized or sequenced under two different isolated conditions, frequently exposes opportunities.

For example, a division sales manager's report of a trip with a salesman contains a chart in which the full scope of the salesman's performance is broken down into elements. Each element of the salesman's performance is rated numerically by the division sales manager. In addition, the division sales manager turns in a descriptive report on the operations of the salesman. In this report the full scope of the salesman's performance is broken down in another manner.

A parallel comparison of the material in the chart with the material in the descriptive outline should expose some possible opportunities. Before this parallel comparison is made, however, the sequence of material in each breakdown pattern should be identical to similar material in the other. Comparables must be aligned so there will be a consecutive consistency between the parallel components.

It is fundamental to the control of results to compare planned or estimated results with actual results. Not many years ago at Williamson-Dickie, excessive inventories and shortages developed from purchasing raw materials based upon inaccurate sales estimates. These sales estimates had been prepared with great care and detail, and several months later results were reported in detail. The sales estimate figures, however, were rarely compared with the results figures except in a general way. Experience brought about an appreciation for this basic requirement of control. Executives now make it a point to emphasize the comparison of these entries.

The main thing to guard against is the failure to compare entries. It is wasteful for costly, carefully prepared estimates to be neglected and gather dust in some pigeonhole while only equally costly records of actual results are studied.

R 3–3: Break Down Deviations

A pattern of prospective results ordinarily is established when plans are determined, but actual deviations from this pattern are not available until the point when the cycle of item advancement is completed. A *deviation* is the extent to which a result varies from a plan. Deviations are known by other terms; such as variations, differences, and disparities. The executive looks for these deviations as well as their opposites—conformities and correspondences.

After comparing entries of plans with results, the executive breaks down the deviations revealed. He does this by developing a list of subheadings that provide an arrangement common to both plans and results. To *break down* is to analyze a collection of content material.

This dissection or division points out trouble spots or areas of opportunity in the deviations. The combined deviation not broken down is only useful to point out the seriousness of the total deviation.

When the executive examines a report, his usual aim is to locate without undue delay the most useful operating information. To accomplish this he may unsystematically review the report until he intuitively senses what appears to be an opportunity, a technique which does not furnish much guidance for executive trainees. On the other hand, if he starts with Item 1 and tries to proceed consecutively through to Item 30, he probably will run out of time long before he finishes.

An alternative to this approach would be to select some outstanding or flagrant deviation on the operating statement—such as supplies—even though this item might constitute only 1/20th of the area of the full scope. Another time-saving, although not always applicable, approach is to start with the full scope. In this approach, the first segment examined for deviations on the Monthly Operating Statement would be the total net profit. If the report were the Balance Sheet, the starting segment to examine would be the total net worth.

A results review of a major item such as the operating statement should continue until deviations are broken down to a smaller area which will still retain a pattern of accountability or responsibility. To insure this, such a breakdown or reduction scheme of results and deviation should parallel the organization structure, as far as convenient, to reflect the responsibility or accountability for each breakdown. In this way, when areas with the greatest opportunity or deviation are exposed, they can be tied-in directly with a single responsibility center.

R 3–4: Compute Indexes

Figures may be used effectively to express results, especially when the figures are comparable. To be comparable, however, they usually must be reduced to index figures or operating averages.

An *index* is a ratio or other number derived from a series of observations and used as an indicator or measure of a certain condition. An average is a commonly used index representing the ordinary experience. A simple arithmetical average or mean is determined by dividing the sum or total of all the quantities by their number. "Per cent of net sales," "per cent of direct labor," and "hours per one hundred units" are all examples of indexes.

Indexes must be computed, calculated, or figured, since they generally must be more definite than figures produced by an estimate, guess, or speculation.

Index figures can be used as gauges in evaluating a production line's performance: by comparing its standard cycle with the actual cycle time of the operation. For example, .63 minutes may be the standard cycle time for a two-machine operation, while the actual cycle time may be 1.09 minutes. Dividing .63 by 1.09 results in an index of 57.8 per cent—an indication of the relative efficiency of the operation under study.

EOT as a whole might be thought of as a pattern of analysis, but this chapter has been attending to the guide points which bear particularly on Analysis of Relationships. In the consideration of these, multiple purposes appear. Guides to their coordination are the concern of the next chapter.

VII

Coordinating Purposes

Purposes are definite intentions or designs to attain a desired effect. They are the things to be done or attained; that is, objects in view, intended results, or aims. These purposes are more pointed than plans, although it is typical to have a purpose in mind before a definite plan is formulated.

A purpose also may be less mature than a definite objective. Questions such as these are frequently used to identify purpose:

"Why are we together?"
"What are we trying to do?"

Purpose should be kept in mind throughout an advancement cycle so that steps taken will be relevant to it. This makes the best of one's efforts and energies. For this reason, individuals contemplating a course of action should state their purpose. They should declare what the proposed action will accomplish or contribute. Since other individuals are involved, the need arises for mutual identification and coordination of purposes.

Possible purposes may be suggested by using the EOT emphasis areas and guide points to classify a particular action or intended action. The verbs suggest purpose, while the nouns indicate usefulness.

Another way to delineate purpose is to translate the results of the intended action into benefits. Identifying the purpose of the intended action may involve the separation of the means from the end. This "end," when clarified and expressed as a tangible or logical benefit to the situation furnishes a rational basis for action.

Several years ago an executive desired to add a new model to the Williamson-Dickie line which involved adding both another make and another cloth. When the purpose was analyzed, the disadvantages outweighed the benefits. In this case the intention to add the new model had been conceived merely because someone had asked for the model and it appeared consistent with the existing line. There was no rational basis for action.

Purposes are frequently intuitive, and unless there is a consciousness of purpose, emotions alone may control action. Such action has no logically beneficial basis.

Purpose is more frequently applied to and certainly is easier to visualize in areas of narrow scope. It is just as necessary, however, to apply it to the broad, company-wide decisions and policies. The executive often shifts his consideration from remoteness to immediacy in order to provide an immediate purpose as opposed to a more remote intended consequence. Nevertheless, he should coordinate the purpose of a particular intention with that purpose intended by the broad objective of the enterprise.

Coordinate means to place or arrange parts in proper position relative to each other and to the system to which they belong, bringing them into proper combined order. Coordination is acting in combined order for the production of a particular result.

Although the will to coordinate purposes usually is achieved at the Unify Views step, there still remains the process of actual coordination. This means that related action, agents, and operations must be arranged harmoniously and without conflict, so as to favor the production of an intended result. Integrating and organizing allow simultaneous and orderly actions. Dimensionalizing purposes relegates each individual to his proper function.

Actual coordination materializes for better or for worse when action is produced. For interrelated action to move toward a common goal correlative factors must be recognized and acted upon.

EOT includes in coordination the element of time and timing. Time, when referred to in the abstract, may be visualized as an indeterminate void. The real substance of time, as it concerns executives, is the productive activity materializing between the starting and stopping points of the time period. Executives reckon with extent of continuation and endeavor to fit operating events within its limits. These activities may sometimes be measured quantitatively in numbers of units produced or may be measured qualitatively as to usefulness.

Time enters substantially as a consideration in the work day of the executive. He prepares schedules by singling out particular items needing consideration and action during a certain period. This schedule may be interrupted to handle unforeseen matters.

Dealing with time in the future is generally more difficult than dealing with time in the past. Past points and periods of time are quite definite. Their study, however, may yield clues as to utilization of time in the future. Effective management of this future time will yield satisfying results to the executive.

Visualizing time as having definite boundaries is helpful. Time may be bounded by a start and a stop, and the point of time as represented by the date of the start and of the stop must be considered by executives. When the time period's scope is broad enough, a stop may complete a mission and not necessarily complete only one phase of a mission. Visualizing the full focal scope of time suggests finality.

COORDINATING PURPOSES: EXPOSE CONDITIONS

C 4–1: *Investigate Backgrounds*

In an alert organization, the easily observed or self-evident conditions already have been exposed and are in the executive process. Exposing the less obvious conditions calls for further investigation.

The situation should be examined in greater detail. Here the executive investigates, probes, and explores the background of the situation. *Background* is the accumulation of earlier conditions or events which help to explain later conditions or events.

Unlike those in the better lighted foreground, background conditions require intensive investigation, as a rule. The executive's *investigation* is a systematic trackdown of conditions he hopes to discover and needs to know. It is an exhaustive inquiry. He should not overlook any characteristic or any object of the situation which may yield helpful conditions.

Every technique of investigation may be utilized at this point. Although some significant conditions are disclosed accidentally, others are revealed only by careful investigation of controllable areas such as quantity, quality, costs, and time.

The personnel executive investigates backgrounds when he checks references to determine a candidate's experience, knowledge, and training. The credit executive utilizes this technique when he thoroughly checks a prospective account's credit standing and his paying records. His investigation may be even more intensive if the account has a high fire loss record, for example. The president usually makes an exhaustive investigation of a firm's history and evolutionary development in addition to financial records when he is contemplating its purchase.

Some careless executives misapply their confidence. They believe people "who are supposed to know." They sometimes blindly believe a person of prestige and do not bother to investigate his correctness. Others blindly follow "sacred cows" of outmoded conventions, traditions, and mores.

C 4–2: *Start Preliminaries*

Some developments in a situation may indicate that the time to start the item may be "now or never." Other developments may indicate starting now is untimely, and that the start should be postponed. The workloads of others have a bearing on this matter of tying on to the time chain at the right spot. Deadline requirements are also important; such as being ready in time to catch a production line run, or the closing deadline of a seasonal product line. Sometimes a matter is so important that it needs to be started at once, whether everyone concerned is ready or not.

The executive can draw on many skills to advance items; but he is sometimes hampered by lack of time. Seasoned executives expect the unforeseen delays which their experience tells them customarily appear. It is important, therefore, to look ahead for details which should be handled ahead of the main item.

Work on these preliminaries or preparatory steps should be set in motion far enough in advance of other intended actions to provide ample time for completion. With preparation complete, the critical actions will be simpler to handle and the executive is more likely to meet his action deadline. Being early is often an advantage, whereas being late may weigh even greater as a disadvantage. The executive has time to exploit the creative by-products of discussions if as many preliminaries as possible have been disposed of.

In 1956, Williamson-Dickie's Research Director developed a spring and fall merchandise line schedule. This schedule, which continued for several seasons, provided that designing should be started in April for the next spring line to coincide with the textile mills' schedules. The mills offer new cloths in May and June for the following spring season. Since each spring line is presented and issued to the salesmen in September or October, this allowed only three or four months to completely design a new line. In seeking to improve the effectiveness of the spring line designing, development of the spring line makes was started in January. Development of cloths was scheduled to fit in with the readiness of the mills to disclose their new cloth ideas as early in May and June as possible.

Starting these preliminaries early enabled Williamson-Dickie to meet the September deadline with a better designed product line.

C 4–3: *Arrange Facilities*

When an undertaking is started into operation, a principal deterrent to advancement is that certain essential facilities are not available for use.

These facilities may be the written material or reports which must be available if the executive is to proceed easily in advancing the item. The particulars of this material must be conveniently indexed and organized.

The time required to arrange for these facilities or equipment often does not appear to be directly productive, but this is a necessary step to the undertaking. This arrangement may be an even larger job than the undertaking itself. For that reason the executive may find a procedural step-by-step approach feasible. He must realize, however, that overrefinement of detail at this point may actually delay rather than speed item advancement.

Equipment is another type of facility that must be arranged in advance. In 1959, an experimental project for bonding shirt cuffs and pocket flaps with synthetic resin film was delayed several months because a special press had not yet been purchased.

When the executive has recourse to facilities or conveniences, time and energy required to produce results will be reduced. The absence of facilities may be a handicap which is virtually impossible to overcome without more time than is available.

C 4–4: Date Progressions

Progression is the improvement, movement forward, or headway that may be expected from action steps. This consideration was recognized early in the development of EOT and was called Progress Status.

Progress status was the result of a continuous advancement or forward movement toward a set objective. It stressed the distances covered, the changes that had taken place, and the amount of improvement made. The present EOT concept considers, with progression, the date of a happening or the point of time on which a specific event has or will transpire.

A *date* is the point of time at which an event takes place or is appointed to take place. The executive activity of dating progressions includes finding out the date of, giving a date to, or marking with a date.

When an executive asks, "When is the break-off point of this record?" or "When do conditions require that we start?" he is endeavoring to set a date. The relative time of occurrence between two different events is also worthwhile to consider, and the dates of these happenings usually should be ascertained and specified. Whether a happening occurred recently or some time ago is also an important consideration.

The dating of past happenings or changes may not be as difficult as dating possible future progressions or improvements. In dealing with the future, the executive needs to anticipate conditions from which may arise unforeseen coordination defects. These planned future events should be dated as to when they are expected to occur.

The executive may need to be in two cities 1,000 miles apart at the same time. Because of the difficulty of fitting together these purposes, he may procrastinate in dating future happenings. A procrastinating executive also may be fully determined to start an advancement effort, but he has never decided exactly when. Deciding when to start an item may also involve facing present needs.

Conditions such as needs or availability will have dates of probable materialization which the executive should note. As the advancement effort proceeds, the executive should compare these notes with materialized progressions. Omissions, insufficiencies, or the lack of progress by the due date probably will be more important to him than the simple fact that happenings or some progress occurred.

Senior executives at Williamson-Dickie can follow progressions by reading weekly activity reports. These are written narratives in which each executive records his activities during the week reported. The executive who is aggressively striving to advance items under his responsibility willingly reports their status in his report. At other times he is able to report verbally on their progress when called upon.

One important point the executive should keep in mind is that situations may deteriorate with the passage of time unless the action indicated is taken at an early date.

COORDINATING PURPOSES: DEVELOP IDEAS

I 4-1: Perceive Time Openings

Dealing with time would be simpler if each executive could stay on one item or step until he finishes it. But time seldom permits this. Thus an awareness of available time to participate in daily operations is essential to the executive.

An executive must be on the lookout for available time opportunities that will allow sufficient time to complete a cycle of work. This cycle of work is expected to yield results or at least should indicate that tangible results will be forthcoming.

Estimating the time each executive activity will consume is almost impossible. Nevertheless, the executive can arrange his planned activities in sequence of expected handling. He also must watch for the opportunity to combine another item with a current undertaking. Circumstances sometimes arise unexpectedly which permit a more favorable utilization of time than the planned sequence. A capable executive observes and responds to such developments. He may eliminate or delay for later consideration untimely material in order to provide an appropriate time opening.

An unskilled executive, on the other hand, frequently handicaps the advancement of his item by causing untimeliness to work against him. He may start actions in motion at an inopportune time. They may be premature moves or intrusions, or they may be actions started after the opportune time is past.

In the continuity of executive operations, there are points in the action cycle in which an appropriate termination has been approached. An executive seeks to perceive these cycle endings so they may be used as stopping points. These timing opportunities are very closely related to next steps.

Much of the coordination in executive operations is handled on an intuitive basis. The executive senses opportunities for tuning in or out of an item or area. The executive's answer to the question "When is the best time to do it?" sometimes suggests a time opening.

Near the fiscal year end in June, 1959, Williamson-Dickie's General Sales Manager observed that stocks were low on the most popular slacks. Size ranges were broken at each of the five regional warehouses. Knowing that the truck fleet would be returning empty to Fort Worth after the June 30th inventory, he capitalized upon this opportune time to combine all stocks for better utilization of sizes. Until stocks were exhausted, the central warehouse delivered to customers a more complete range of sizes than would have been possible from the regional warehouses. This flexibility did not add to total costs.

Watching for time openings does not mean being shortsighted or opportunistic. The executive needs to keep the short range in direct view, but he needs to have the long-range benefits in the back of his mind. In the case just mentioned, such a condition could develop. Maintaining only one central stock when supplies are ample, for example, could slow deliveries to customers.

Merchandising decisions frequently involve the opportune nature of time openings. The axiom "Climb on fast with more merchandise and climb off fast with liquidations," calls for this type of intuitive thinking.

Time is frequently wasted by carrying a discussion beyond its useful stopping point. Many salesmen have had the experience of "talking" themselves out of a sale by carrying the sales talk on so far beyond the point needed for conviction that the buyer changes his mind. The executive needs to recognize the point of diminishing returns in a conference and voluntarily turn the discussion to other areas of opportunity. Some stopping points, of course, are involuntary. They are brought about by interruptions, emergencies, visitors, telephone calls, and other external influences.

I 4–2: Pace Assimilations

Assimilations are changes absorbed within an organization during a given period of time. The executive group should pace assimilations at a speed which will advance the item. Each member shares responsibility for satisfactory progression of the item. They should not permit assimilation of operations to slow to an unsatisfactory pace. On the other hand, their responsibility also is to report unfavorable effects if the item is being carried too fast.

The rate of advancement is governed to some extent by the assimilation capacity of the individuals involved. For this reason changes should not be put into effect faster than the group or operation can absorb them. Another caution is to be careful of starting new items when the schedule is overloaded with older, but just as important items.

The coordinating executive should balance between insistence on acceleration and patience. His job is to speed assimilation to a satisfactory advancement speed, but without attempting to move the item too fast. Not only can he carry others too fast, but he may try to carry himself too fast. This excessive pace causes only confusion, especially when the executive leaves ordinary reminders and tries to take nonexistent shortcuts.

Some selected areas justify extra emphasis and adaptation for assimilation. The executive should allow extra time on these for the maturing of attitudes and the perspective needed.

The executive must control his involvement in any particular item. If he attempts, for example, to take over an item and carry the ball, he may find that the item will not advance at all during the interval between his own item advancement efforts. Thus, he may find that he has insufficient time to justify such an arrangement. Items and undertakings can grow in complexity and scope. This also affects the number of items and undertakings an executive personally handles.

Executives are faced with the problem of resolving several conflicting requirements as to the allocation of his time and effort. Certain types of items and functions are subject to scheduling daily, weekly, monthly, or quarterly, an executive consideration discussed later in this chapter. In developing schedules the executive considers the number of items to schedule in one day, the possible time to be spent on each item, and the total number of items he can keep in touch with.

Another time consideration is the length of an item conference. A conference should be long enough to disclose enough operating material to generate clues to advancement. On the other hand a conference can consume valuable time that might be used on other items to better advantage. Some executives feel that a conference continued beyond two hours is likely to go into unproductive time.

I 4–3: Incubate Refinements

After the active effort subsides, ideas frequently are developed during a period of idle reflection. This delayed development should be encouraged by making note of such late emerging ideas. These afterthoughts can result in definite refinements over and beyond those resulting from ordinary time, skill, and effort. They are frequently the slight difference that is the competitive advantage of many firms or products.

The more time a subject is intensively considered, the greater is its development. Memory plays a substantial part in this refinement of ideas. Most ideas are warmed over or incubated inclinations that previously have been in the executive's field of awareness. It is, therefore, consistently to the executive's interest to keep the Develop Ideas step open to take advantage of this incubation—a pondering or mulling over —so as to continue refinement even when there is no intensive advancement effort.

The continuity of time applies to executive effort and emphasis. Some executives may expend an intense effort for a short time. This will then be followed by a decline in interest. Other executives, however, will maintain continuity of emphasis long after a formal item advancement effort has ended. This continuity of emphasis permits the executive to capture afterthoughts that result from a maturing incubation period. Some of the best ideas and deepest insights occur during our more relaxed moments. The executive should expect and enter additional ideas after a conference has been held. His operating techniques should enable him to capture these refinements as normally expected consequences of intensive operations.

I 4–4: Classify Usefuls

The executive reviews the useful material noted in the previous step. He then classifies useful elements by considering their usefulness according to pertinence to the situation or item. Each element of content material has a particular usefulness or materiality in executive operations. On the other hand, extraneous material has little or no utility or relevance.

Usefulness is the capacity of operating material to serve a practical purpose. This usefulness is usually designated by the EOT Executive Considerations, Advancement Steps, or guide points.

The best executives, it has been said, work with the most useful or relevant material. Familiarity with EOT permits executives to carefully classify such usefulness, to sort out, to distinguish, and to group. Intermingled, misclassified, or unclassified material renders all the material unusable. For example, each topic or content element discussed in an item conference is usually classified—either formally or subconsciously —as to its usefulness.

Just as identifying questions and actions by purpose is a typical operating activity, it is important to identify the usefulness of operating material. A purpose seems to imply an intended action. By contrast, something at rest (such as an element of executive material) is passive and sterile as to purpose. Such material, however, may have usefulness which is helpful in identifying.

COORDINATING PURPOSES: UNIFY VIEWS

V 4-1: *Continue Contacts*

Contacts are meetings between two or more individuals in which the object is to discuss or handle a situation of mutual interest. Previous personal contact conditions individuals for unification of views. A group of people regularly working together and jointly participating, usually reach a plateau of favorable teamwork relationship.

Even when individuals have established this effective working relationship, however, the contact will usually lapse unless it is continued by conscious effort. Interest is also likely to decline when the novelty wears off or when difficult obstacles are met.

Contacts, especially when people have never worked together, will probably become easier to maintain as the individuals gain confidence in the judgment of others. If individuals are given an opportunity to "blow off steam," or to get complaints "off their chests," constructive contacts in subsequent meetings are more likely.

Memory and acquaintances help to build a contact background. This background is developed by the frequency of contacts, the length of time the relationship has been established, the nature of the contacts, and the individual requirements of the joint efforts.

In continuing contacts, the time factor aids the executive in maintaining good working relationships with his co-workers. Maintaining a continuity of topical content from one conference or contact to another uses past established relationships to advantage. The junior executive should feel that the senior is always available to him for consultation.

On the other hand, the senior executive should feel that he can make a casual inquiry about the progress of an item without causing a junior to feel his senior is "breathing down my neck." Established institutions, seniority, and tried-and-proved methods are all related to this concept of spending time to continue contacts.

In a sales situation the salesman gains the favorable attention of his prospective customer by continued contacts. The executive also needs to consider this factor when he is presenting a proposal.

If others benefit by being in contact with an individual, they are more likely to look on him with favor. Any service he renders advances good will toward him. Favors he does for people make them like him.

V 4–2: Tie-in Transitions

In any project or organization the executive needs to develop and preserve a continuity between the related factors of an item or operation. Activities should be linked, so that when one stops, the next will start without unnecessary overlaps, duplications, or skips which would otherwise remain unhandled. A transition is the juncture at which one activity, topic, or responsibility passes from one phase or individual to another.

To *tie-in* means to link, connect, or bring together two or more separate activities or efforts in order to carry them out consecutively without breaking continuity. Someone must couple or link these steps; otherwise, there will be a break and the activity will not continue. The item needs to be handed from one executive to the other as a relay runner passes the baton on to his teammate. An item sometimes stops when an executive comes to a point where a decision is needed to keep the item advancing. To start the item moving again, seniors or associates usually have to intervene.

A *tied-in transition* is an indication of continuity in coordination. The transmissions or change-overs of responsibilty may be both formal and informal. The transition between functional assignments, such as between production and sales, is more evident than one between junior and senior. It is the executive's function to tie-in every assignment or determination of a next step at the end of an item conference.

Someone has to "carry the ball," and each key executive must guard against habitually offering to carry the ball himself. This discourages other executives from carrying it.

Tied-in transitions preserve the continuity and effective flow of operations and thereby prevent executives from "losing their places." In the same way, proper indexes in a note file mark the last point reached. That point can then be picked up to start successive advancement efforts.

V 4–3: Accept Responsibilities

The fundamental purpose in passing the baton of action from one executive to another is coordinated advancement efforts upon the item. Although perspectives may differ, each executive has a responsibility for advancing the item. When items are created from a situation fully understood and accepted by each, the focal point is the entire situation and not some aspect of the situation with which one or the other becomes absorbed.

Item advancement, then, is the central concern that should be shared by all members of the cooperating group. Each executive should accept the accountability for items or next steps assigned to him. This acceptance of responsibility implies an agreement or understanding to produce action under reasonably expected conditions. It is made with adequate realization and balance of the factors of time, quality, quantity, and cost. When the entire group is unified on this foundation, they are in position to go into the final step before action—Determine Plans.

Accepting responsibility implies that the receiver approves the action connotated and that he has no undisclosed reservations regarding it. Nevertheless, the key executive must make sure that he has secured acceptance of the assignment by the junior executive. If this is not done, the key executive may find that the item advances only when he personally works with it.

When the senior executive coordinates action by holding an item himself and delegating next steps, the junior leaves responsibility for action to the senior all too frequently. The problem facing the executive organization here is how to coordinate the activity of the junior executive with the immediate situation's needs, without the senior executive still holding the reins.

Failure of certain executives in a cooperating group to accept responsibility for their undertakings noticeably affects the company's progress. If only one individual fails to complete his assignments, both the item and the group effort are delayed or stopped. But when every executive accepts his responsibilities, the item advances in easy stages of delegated, cooperative advancement and orderly reporting or review. Eventually the entire item can be released to the functional responsibility of junior executives.

A large part of the responsibility expected of executives is tied into schedule awareness as time requirements vitally affect the advancement of the item. This schedule responsibility is the feeling which impels the executive to be concerned about the time planned events will probably happen or be completed.

V 4-4: Build Permanencies

For efforts to yield satisfactory results, solutions should be reasonably stable or permanent. A problem situation temporarily or incompletely solved may confront the executive in more serious form at a later date. The executive, therefore, should build the solution substantially and securely, so that it will be effective as long as it is needed. Time is a consideration at this point both from the standpoint of time required to achieve a permanent solution and from the length of time the solution will endure.

Executives should cultivate a perspective of thinking in terms of long-range improvements and developments. Training employees and drafting policies are examples of permanent improvements rather than temporary solutions. In other words, the executive senses the distinction between taking aspirin and pulling the tooth. This does not mean, however, that permanent solutions may not be built on a step-by-step basis.

Observing and following broad movements and influences contributes to more permanent solutions. Ignoring a trend of circumstances that can likely erase the result of efforts may cause the solution to fail the test of time.

COORDINATING PURPOSES: DETERMINE PLANS

P 4-1: Sequence Efforts

Efforts or, more precisely, *item advancement efforts* are actions by which executives endeavor to advance an undertaken item to a more nearly complete status. These progression periods are segments of time in which effort is being expended by the executive. These efforts should be sequenced to the best advantage. In sequencing, executives arrange undertakings or topics in order of expected chronological succession. They place them in the order to which they expect to be able to devote time and attention to them. This activity is called scheduling or programming.

In *sequencing efforts* the executive sets up the points of the previously analyzed situation in a chronological sequence. In this way the executive will know the next thing to handle, whether it be an objective, project, item, step, or other emphasized area.

It is usually helpful to avoid evaluation and arrangement of facts too early. A random listing that has no logical significance (such as alphabetical order) is a satisfactory preliminary to sequencing.

Sequencing advancement efforts schedules the expenditure of executive time in the future. If the usual EOT Pattern has been followed, the sequencing of efforts has been preceded by many emphasizd considerations and handled steps. Later the guide point P 6–2, Rank Selections, may suggest a basis for sequencing efforts. More than mere importance, other criteria must be taken into consideration. Timeliness, effort required to finish, and ease to handle through delegation are some of the other considerations.

Adequate sequencing reflects a type of executive skill and is tied in closely with timing needs. This skill differs in executives and also in the same executive at the start of his career, and later in life. It *involves the ability to consider the interrelationship of many factors without losing the visualization and intellectual control of the whole.*

A schedule of efforts is not necessarily rigid, but it does give the executive a schedule to work against, and eliminates ambiguity in deciding what to handle next. If some flexibility is used at the start of sequencing and if the material has been worked with to gain familiarity, the elements are likely to fall into place without undue forcing.

An agenda presupposes that topics listed are sequenced in order of logical convenience for discussion. A typical method of handling an agenda is to start with the first topic and endeavor to discuss the topics in the order they appear on the agenda. In a spirited and effective discussion some topics may be spontaneously developed ahead of their planned order. It then becomes the choice of the chairman to restrict or permit the discussion of this spontaneous topic. Following the latter course frequently preserves participation without losing time. Then when the prematurely handled topic does appear on the agenda, it may be passed over and used only as a reminder to the conference chairman.

When the items of a day are being scheduled, one problem is the relation between expected results from the item advancement effort and the possible time available to spend on the item. This involves a dual awareness of the full scope of the day's scheduling along with the need for emphasis upon the current item.

Few items can be pushed all the way to a conclusion in one effort. Usually they are delayed to make progress on other items. This causes executives to be on the lookout for natural stopping places and transition opportunities, so that the next scheduled item may be taken up.

The Item Schedule Procedure illustrated on the following pages was developed in 1952. It represents an exhaustive effort to insure complete attention and follow-through on all items undertaken. At the time of introduction, Williamson-Dickie executives almost universally used this procedure. This intensive scheduling program has been relaxed somewhat. Certainly a larger proportion of the executives are more reliable in reporting progressions. Also, they rely more upon convictions when assignments are given. Items still become lost, however, and need reactivation by top executive levels.

Instead of item cards, some executives enter the item in the left hand margin of their chronological note files. Other entries in need of handling are marked with a short horizontal line to the left of the entry in the file.

Executives are cautioned to be very critical of an item schedule procedure which does not provide a constant reminder of items to handle. The price paid in effort returns positive benefits in results.

FIGURE 7.

ITEM SCHEDULE PROCEDURE

STEPS		KEY POINTS	
1	Enter all items on cards.	101	Include routine, operating, educational, and developmental items.
		102	Include items you handle yourself, as well as items to review and report.
		103	Write new or unforeseen items scheduled during day on schedule sheet and write cards if carried over.
11	Designate person to handle item within lower left hand corner of card.	1101	Number and initial (or use abbreviation).
2	Arrange all item cards in Schedufile.		

STEPS	KEY POINTS
21 Arrange cards scheduled for current week's attention.	2101 Arrange items first by major reporting function and then in order of sequence to be handled.
	2102 Put cards in top of card holder for day of week scheduled, above the functional grouping.
	2103 Transfer today's cards to "today's" card holder.
22 Arrange nonscheduled cards by person with whom you expect to handle. (See 4202)	2201 Reduce scope content of item, so may be handled by one person if practicable.
	2202 Distribute items uniformly between persons if possible.
3 Arrange today's schedule in sequence in today's card holder.	301 Arrange items by reporting function and in order of sequence to be handled.
31 Type today's schedule.	3101 Date schedule and identify with your name.
	3102 Triple space between items.
	3103 Items on left side of sheet to allow notation space.
4 Mark up schedule.	401 X before items completed.
	/ Progression sign before items which were advanced.
	C before items carried over or not reached.
41 Remove handled cards from today's card holder at end of day.	
42 Arrange cards scheduled for later attention and follow up.	4201 Cards for current week in top of card holder for day of week scheduled.
	4202 Group cards beyond current week by function and person with whom you expect to handle.

STEPS	KEY POINTS
5 Coordinate your schedule with reporting and reviewing chairman.	501 Match levels of scope.
	502 Each item in reviewer's schedule should be represented by card in reporter's schedule.
51 Coordinate views of reviewer and reporter on value arrangement of item cards.	

P 4–2: Synchronize Schedules

A *schedule* is a disposition in advance of the time advancement efforts are intended to be applied to items undertaken by an individual within a customary work period. In sequencing, the individual executive sets up his own scheduling. Unless schedules of everyone involved are synchronized before the time of action, it may be found that executives are not available. They are out of town or out of the office, causing delay in the item advancement, or disruption of individual schedules. For this reason executives should be familiar with the schedules of others. Item advancement efforts can then be scheduled at suitable and convenient times for all involved.

To *synchronize* means to establish dates and durations of occurrence of two or more expected activities in such a way that they will harmonize and contribute to a common end. The attitude of time awareness should be shared by members of the operating group. All involved should feel the need for a unified coordinating intelligence in which the group participates. Members of the group should know and coordinate the sequence characteristics and relative time requirements of their recommendations, approvals, and reviews. Questions such as "Shall we tell him June 1?" and "When do we plan to have this program completed?" involve setting a deadline. The purpose of these deadlines is frequently to plan personal schedules in providing for coordinated or near-simultaneous completions.

Coordination of time leads us into a study of the duration of the item advancement efforts of different individuals in the group. How a single executive may, with a working degree of effectiveness, schedule his day's work has been discussed. In a group, it is necessary to coordinate the efforts of several in order to attain a minimum of wasted effort. Conferences bring together the item advancement efforts of several individuals at the same time. Advancement status of each related item or sub-item affects and alters the timeliness and urgency of other items. Such undertakings should be handled with good judgment. Otherwise they will become so ponderous as to lose rather than save time.

Individuals may agree on the merits of an undertaken item. When a decision as to time to schedule is required, other important items may be scheduled by those involved. A suitable time opening must be found that will enable each individual concerned to fit his participation on this item into his own time schedule. In making decisions as to timing of action, one of the early things to consider is the sequence priority. What is the probability of the time available to devote to the advancement efforts?

This consideration of timing, timeliness, and acting when the time is right, and avoiding untimely starts which retard progress, involves the consideration of many individuals and factors. The value of possible results should be weighed in advance against the time available or required.

P 4–3: Proceduralize Routines

Executives repeatedly deal with plans in some form. Much of their energy is required to adapt these plans for guides to action and results. Even after views have been unified or alternatives have been developed, a plan must be reduced to a degree of definiteness suitable for action. Having stood the test of subjective views, it must be constructed to withstand the stresses of objective action.

A *routine* is a form of plan which has been adopted to guide action. It is a fixed, regular method of doing things. Certain types of repetitive activities are susceptible to developing into a routine. To be effective, these routines should be followed in steps and in a definite order. They should not require complex judgment.

Since a routine is often followed by many individuals, *proceduralizing* such routines helps executive operations. This means to describe and divide routine activities into a series of interrelated steps, the series having a definite beginning and end. This arrangement will guide individuals in conducting similar recurring activities.

Any pattern of activity used consciously and repeatedly may be formalized into such a procedure and become a part of an inventory or stock of plans. The six questions—What?, Why?, When?, How?, Where?, and Who?—by this interpretation form a simple procedure.

An effective working procedure helps to maintain interest through action. "Making a game of it" helps add interest to any situation by mixing "how" with "what." Following this cycle of experience is "training through doing," rather than "training through telling."

The process of proceduralizing usually starts with observing the entire scope of an activity in its initial random, *de facto*, or unanalyzed condition. The process may be compared with an hourglass pattern, following the three steps:

1. Introduction and overall picture,
2. Consideration of each separate content element, and
3. Summary and conclusion of the full scope of the situation.

Thus, the finished procedure is the base of the hourglass, Step 3.

There are several degrees of formality in proceduralization. One of the simplest procedures is to list in pencil on an alphabetical sheet the content elements of a situation as they occur, and then to sequence them by number in any order preferred. Any subsequent entries may be entered in proper alphabetical position and worked into the sequence by assigning letters to numbers already chosen. For example, if Elements No. 1, 2, 3, 4, and 5 were listed, and two other content elements are later inserted, they may fall between those numbered 3 and 4. These new elements may then be called 3A and 3B, which would preserve the sequence desired without repositioning any of the entries. More formal procedures with steps and key points can be developed where the frequency of use justifies.

In certain cases, several executives may share the effort to advance an item, alternating as the key executive. Thus at different times different individuals may "carry the ball." The listing of content elements in sequence is a useful technique in these cases. Individual personalities and experience vary. When disclosing new information or when facing new immediate needs, individuals will express and organize the content of a situation somewhat differently. They will also sequence their own content elements differently.

Coordination of executives in such a situation is aided if one controlling topical sequence is followed, irrespective of differences in content of the individual executives' notes. In this way the sequence will agree, even though different individuals might use a different amount of space or number of entries for their topical notes. This sequence will suggest combinations and groupings of topics as opportunities to proceduralize. This interrelated type of handling may increase the amount of material, but it coordinates the work of the executive group. It reduces the need to halt and go through the time-consuming process of trying to agree on a common outline for the situation.

One advantage of a procedure is evident when the results of an activity are unsatisfactory. Sales estimating, for example, may be inaccurate. An examination of each step of the sales estimating procedure will frequently indicate where the error in estimating originated.

One limitation to proceduralizing nonroutine practices is found in the use of scope. The General Sales Manager may apply the sales estimating procedure to the full scope, forecasting sales in total garments. His assistant who is developing the sales estimate could apply the same procedure to one of several hundred lot numbers. But it takes considerable time to repeat this procedure for each lot number several hundred times. Time limitation, therefore, calls for selective stratification of the elements in a situation, rather than the consistent but time-consuming treatment of one element after the other in a breakdown scheme.

Understanding and awareness of the usefulness and limitations of organizational procedures improve teamwork. Using them produces automatic reminders and dependable control, although individuals must be oriented to their use. Procedures are effective only through wholehearted use and evolutionary refinement by executives familiar with their application in working situations.

P 4–4: Foresee Strategies

Strategy is a broad course of action, intended to produce results as well as to gain an advantage over obstacles. It is determined in advance of objective action. To *foresee* is to know something is likely to happen with reasonable accuracy in advance of its occurrence. It is a function of the executive to picture these planned maneuvers in advance—to foresee strategies. Strategy is usually general enough to cover more than one possible eventuality. The points covered in broad strategy should be policies, broad continuing objectives, or determinations sufficiently broad of application to be observed and followed without modification. Future decisions and long-range plans also may be called strategies. The executive in charge of a particular item should be able to foresee company strategy that may affect the usefulness or importance of the item.

The executive may foresee the intensification of a condition such as the cost-price squeeze which accompanies an economic recession. The trends he foresees may indicate strategies to overcome the handicap or to take advantage of the conditions.

Unless strategies are thought out in advance, the executive probably will be required to act on impulse. Therefore, to avoid hasty and possibly wrong actions, he must cultivate forethought. In doing so he will visualize and respond to oncoming circumstances and involvements. He will emphasize the future, usually along with the present or past. Future strategies will then take on a measure of definiteness and tangibility which is necessary for strategic thinking.

Executive foresight is often intuitive. Certain individuals seem to possess this ability to a greater degree than others. Lack of vision, of course, may limit an executive's ability to foresee the implications of broader items. In such cases, a narrower next step may be his most effective scope. Williamson-Dickie measures the vision, imagination, and foresight of executive candidates with a Johnson O'Connor test for this purpose. Skill in foresight can be consciously developed by the executive himself.

Questions such as the following are intended to bring out such expectancies: "What are the main obstacles we are likely to run into?" and "Is anything likely to develop we do not now foresee?"

COORDINATING PURPOSES: PRODUCE ACTION

A 4–1: Reconsider Requirements

Requirements are conditions necessary to the success of an undertaking, the handling of which will occupy time and energy of the executive. To *reconsider* is to reexamine previously made conclusions in the light of current requirements of the situation. The executive should not ignore or stand firm upon his old assumptions. He needs to redetermine the requirements at this point.

When action materializes further within a situation, unanticipated obstacles and delays often prevent the executive from carrying out visualized steps. Many refinements frequently take longer than anticipated. On the other hand some actions frequently take less time than anticipated. The latter frees some time which may be filled with productive activity, if the proper alternatives are immediately available.

This constant materializing of events in a different pattern from that visualized causes the executive to reconsider continuously the requirements of the situation. When reconsidering, he must fit the requirements of the time available to the difficulties met and to the opportunities uncovered. Frequently, he must change tactics. Some requirements materialize which have not been foreseen at all. They also need to be considered. The time requirement underlies every consideration at this step. Certain areas may justify more or less time than visualized. As the events of the executive's day unfold, certain scheduled items have been reached and handled, becoming past realities; some are yet to be dealt with. Matching the time with the remaining scheduled work often becomes a critical consideration. Some items may need to be carried over if time runs out.

The hours of time available to any one individual are limited. On the other hand, one individual often does not have the skill to complete an item to his satisfaction in the available time. He must, therefore, multiply either his skill or his hours. From this it can be deduced that *Hours* $\times$ *Skill* $=$ *Results*. One way he can multiply hours is to arrange for other individuals to cooperate in handling situations. This can be accomplished by assigning some part of the item to others. A greater number of individuals consequently can act as an agency for satisfying the time requirement for achievement entirely apart from improving their skills.

A 4–2: Move Back Emphasis Area

Following the executive's reconsideration, he may need to change tactics to bring them into conformity with current developments and needs. He should reset the course and not ignore current developments and blindly maintain a previously set course.

This occasion demands backtracking the emphasis area. The executive should backtrack with full knowledge that he is moving back to an earlier step or consideration. Emphasis areas are EOT steps, considerations, or guide points to which effort is directed. They are the areas of concentration or focal points. We previously have discussed interpreting the assignment. This assignment is the emphasis area within the situation.

Up to this time emphasis has been moving forward, advancing the EOT cycle. In moving back the emphasis area, it becomes necessary for the executive to return the focal point of emphasis or action to an earlier step in the cycle of chronological development or to a less mature point in the depth of development of consideration—in other words, to drop back, to backtrack, or to reverse himself.

The reason for turning back is that the item advancement effort has not been productive. The steps handled or previously emphasized were inadequately performed. Deficient ideas, invalid conditions, and serious divergence of views are all examples of inadequacies which suggest the need for moving back emphasis areas in the EOT Chart so that current emphasis may be applied where needed.

The planned sequence of steps may be re-examined to uncover opportunities for realignment. Resequencing may suggest new combinations or groupings. Certain possible actions if taken immediately may be more productive of advancement than those previously visualized.

This does not mean that the executive should be over-critical and insist on over-refinements. The executive should Utilize Availables if possible to work with what he has. If he does not do this, he is likely to move back unwisely into earlier steps and spend too much time in preparation and too little in execution.

A 4–3: *Activate Idlers*

Items assigned to executives do not always move smoothly and continuously through an advancement cycle to completion. More often, the larger items progress by fits and starts, halting as obstacles are encountered and leaping forward when heavy executive pressure is brought to bear. If an executive relaxes or diverts the attention an item requires, it will frequently become an idle item or *idler*. To activate an idler, the executive must once again turn his exclusive efforts to forcing the item to advance.

Activating idlers should be an everyday concern of the executive. The senior executive can often activate an item he has assigned by merely asking the responsible executive for a report on the item's advancement. In other instances, the executive must clear the obstacles from an item's path by establishing new priorities, suggesting novel approaches, or emphasizing the fundamental techniques of item advancement. For the moment, he must concentrate upon reviving the item from its inactive or lethargic state.

Sometimes an item becomes idle because the executive has not clearly defined the next step. If possible, he should lay out a firm sequence of "next steps" to follow. By doing this, he may avoid the necessity of activating an idle item again and again. Of course, time schedules for completing the series of steps must be made explicit, even if the executive anticipates the probable necessity for later revision.

Many organizations suffer because their executives allow undertaken items to experience unnecessary delay because of neglect. If an item is idle, it is no longer beneficial to the firm, and prior costs already embodied in the item are losses. At regular intervals, responsible executives should critically examine the action status of each item to assure that advancement efforts are continuing to result in progress. If executives view items as the vehicles by which extraordinary beneficial results are obtained for the company, they will devote redoubled efforts to insuring continuous advances.

A 4–4: Meet Deadlines

Deadlines are points of time previously fixed as the latest time for a completion of action. They are dates due, time due, or time limits. Financial obligations are deadlines familiar to all as to their time requirements. Other everyday examples are the times set for appointments and conferences.

Successful executives are accustomed to completing actions at a time previously designated. They customarily work against time to promptly attain time goals. Some executives needlessly postpone their discharge of obligation. These men show little time awareness. Executives need to develop a time awareness, a recognition of the needs and passage of time with respect to the time requirements of their work. Successful executives customarily meet deadlines. Ordinary visiting is enjoyable but tends to waste productive time.

Certain items frequently consume more time than planned. When these items are linked with other coordinated activities the tardy action generally multiplies unfavorable consequences. Such delays may alter the relative priority of parts of a project.

Determination of time priority depends upon current usefulness. Executives with a keen sense of time responsibility respond vigorously to a possible incompatibility between time and the various parts of an undertaking. An executive needs to look ahead to the deadline, considering it continuously until it matures.

One frequent objective is to complete the cycle before time allowed for it runs out. For example, an executive conducting a conference may be about to run out of allowed time, having covered only one-fourth of the agenda. Keeping track of the progress as the action proceeded might have prompted better usage of his time. He can check progress by asking this question: "When one-fourth of our time was consumed, were we one-fourth of the way through the agenda?"

Starting early will relieve much of the pressure to meet a deadline.

COORDINATING PURPOSES: REVIEW RESULTS

R 4–1: Revise Obsoletes

An *obsolete* is a segment of operating material used in the past that is no longer of current status. Out-of-date figures and obsolescent information are included within this definition. Opposites might be the latest available information, updated material, and permanencies. For the sake of drawing valid conclusions, it is necessary to revise obsoletes, bring them up to date, and, if necessary, correct or make them current. Executives frequently must insist upon this revision.

As long as the passage of time exists, executives must expect and adjust obsolescence. Figures that are fresh and potent today are obsolete tomorrow. Executives need to discriminate between the potency of the current figures and those made obsolete by another cut-off date.

Obsolescence is not limited to figures, however, as almost every area of executive operations can deteriorate and lose its value as time passes. These areas include policies and procedures, to name only two. The "m's"—machines, methods, materials, and even money—can become obsolescent or lose their value.

All executives sometimes utilize the latest available information to establish tentative conclusions on a working basis. Nevertheless, as additional information is produced the executive should recognize that this original data has been revised, and that it will be necessary to reconsider his conclusions.

Obsolescence can be evolutionary. A procedure set up for one set of conditions may require periodic revision to changing needs. A business firm can also outgrow members of its staff and line organization. A sales manager whose performance was adequate during a boom period may not succeed in a "hard-sell" depression.

The alert executive recognizes that out-of-date policies may require revision, as such policies may no longer conform to economic necessity. Since its founding in 1922, Williamson-Dickie Manufacturing Company had never altered its policy to operate only within the continental United States. By 1960, however, competition from low labor-cost countries posed a serious threat to the future of domestic men's clothing manufacturers. Many were losing money, and others had been forced to close their doors. Only one United States manufacturer in this field increased its profits substantially that year. This firm had opened a West Indies plant in 1959. Upon reevaluating its policy, Williamson-Dickie's management decided to take offensive action, and in early 1961 opened its first foreign plant. By revising its factory location policy, Williamson-Dickie was ready to meet foreign competition before economic necessity required defensive action.

Programming and scheduling the operations of several manufacturing plants and warehouses usually involves somewhat ponderous procedures and many people. An immediate revision may be indicated by materializing figures. Setting such a revision in motion, however, poses a problem to the executives involved. Should they go through each step of the complex estimating procedure? Or should they provide for informal revisions in the procedure, thus permitting some shortcuts? Pressure of circumstances forces shortcuts occasionally. When such a revision is made, notes should be taken on each step of the shortcut. These notes can later be reviewed profitably for clues to simplifying the procedure.

R 4–2: Check Previous Periods

Previous periods refer to results occurring within a period of time earlier than the presently considered period of the same length. The present period may be one recently ended such as this year, this month, or today. It may be considered while still unexpired. The executive directs his attention toward comparing current results with the previous results. He cannot guess at or disregard results of previous periods, but must refer to and examine this information.

"What was the activity for the previous monthly period? ... for the month before? ... for the same period a year ago?" are questions which refer to results of a previous period. When this information is checked, it supplies the depth of time to figures. Current results may then be visualized in relation to similar results at previous periods. The information gained from checking results of a previous period can serve as a guide for estimates, or it may be a measure of progress.

The information given for each previous period may become more relevant as the information becomes more closely comparable. It is important to know if conditions were the same or similar; for example, if management was increasing or reducing production, or if figures had the same fringe items included. If the incomparability of figures from past periods dilutes their usefulness, then the most current period, the one most recently materialized, may be the most useful.

R 4-3: Detect Trends

Most of the representations that the executive checks with regard to operations are still pictures, so to speak, of a moving situation. He sometimes finds it difficult to visualize continually the changing status of each situation he works with. Nevertheless, he is dealing with a moving target. Just as the hunter aims ahead of a flying bird the executive must "lead" the situation. He does this by detecting trends.

Trends are general courses or patterns of change in the status of a situation. Trends can be revealed by comparing progressive positions of the same performance at successive times. The trend of a situation, inventory, or activity, may be shown by comparing the relative status at one review period to that of several others.

These trends may not be readily discernible. For that reason the executive must discover their existence. He must uncover or reveal them in such a way that understanding and acceptance by others is likely. Trends, therefore, need to be constructed or charted, so that the complexities of their movement is properly revealed to others.

A trend may not be assumed from the change from one period to the next, as a third period may move in another direction and alter this preconception. A valid trend thus needs a series of observations to indicate future expectancies. The duration of the period and the spacing of the intervals are considerations in establishing trends.

Trends may be temporary or one-time. They may be studied if control records provide results in sufficient depth of time to make comparisons.

Trends are especially useful in disclosing progress or deterioration which otherwise would be unnoticed. The trend of a direct labor variance loss continuing over several periods, for example, may be expressed favorably or unfavorably in percentages. The direct labor variance gain may be 5% (of direct labor variance) monthly. Trends may be variations from plans as well as total figures.

Trends may come through growth or deterioration, uninfluenced by executive attention. For this reason, executives detect trends in order to determine whether they are planning with a trend or against it. Progress is faster in areas with favorable trends. Development of time exists whether executives recognize it or not. If they do recognize it, the recognition should materialize in some sort of plan. With a previously set plan in existence, they can take full advantage of the growth and development with time and avoid the deterioration which time often brings about.

R 4–4: *Index References*

References are segments of information, usually in written form, which are accessible in location and arrangement for later attention. Executives frequently memorize these supplements in order to make greater use of their past experience.

Indexing is arranging material in convenient order and marking it by symbols for later reference. The symbols used may be numbers, letters, or dates. The material may be classified within a breakdown scheme and so indexed. Material in several separate locations is more difficult to refer to and work with than if it has all been transferred and entered in one location.

Indexing and cross-indexing take time. If frequently proven useful, however, time and effort expended on indexing is justified.

It is unwise to devote so much time to indexing that it will become an end in itself. For this reason executives at Williamson-Dickie have developed a way to preserve their working notes. The main feature is a chronological note file, in which notes and sheets are accumulated and dated in the order of occurrence and entry. There is a minimum of sorting and classifying of the material, as it is indexed and referred to on a chronological basis. This chronological note file is used to refresh the memories of executives on information discussed and noted at previous conferences. Information relevant to the last discussion will preserve the continuity of the undertaken item. The chronological note procedure is also discussed at the Recall Notations guide point, R 1–3.

Listing entries in alphabetical order furnishes automatic reference. It is sometimes desirable to provide for growth and expansion in the number of entries by allowing several lines of space between entries. This permits later entries to be inserted at the proper location, thus simplifying indexing.

Consideration of purposes and their coordination is always more or less consciously in the mind of the executive. Attention is now directed to the consideration of risks and the control which the executive may exercise to minimize inherent uncertainty and build upon certainties.

VIII

Controlling Certainties

Executives are frequently concerned with the degrees of probability of an expected or possible event. This brings them to the consideration of certainties.

Certainty is the state of being fully confident upon the grounds of knowledge or other facts known to be true. This consideration deals with events which may happen in the future, but it also concerns what happened in the past. The validity of an assumption or the accuracy of a determination may come into question, but certainty is not entirely negative. Positive reliability and faith are favorable ingredients in the success of executive operations.

Certainty may be the most complex, most unpredictable, or most imponderable of the considerations. It is a major factor in judgment, the rarest of executive skills. Much and possibly all authority resides in certainty. It may apply to the full scope of the business enterprise or to an executive career, spanning a lifetime. Thus the control of certainties is a fundamental consideration.

Closely allied with the certainty factor is the activity generally referred to as *controlling*. The executive in controlling uses plans as a supplement to and sometimes in place of his direct, personal influence. These plans must be definitely expressed, delegated, and designed for later review. Determined goals definitely expressed are more susceptible to the activity of control.

The usual narrow definition of controlling needs to be amplified somewhat to accommodate EOT needs. For this purpose, a broader definition of control is using Executive Operations Technique to furnish a definite, factual, inferential, and psychological basis for the steps and considerations leading toward completion of an undertaken item. In this way, controlling may be achieved near the conclusion of each advancement step in the EOT Chart. This assures that the advancement step just completed has been adequately handled. The exposure of conditions, for example, should be fully carried out so as to contribute to advancement toward results by suggesting ideas to develop. In this way the acquisition of certainty increases and enhances as the advancement steps materialize within an item.

With adequate skill in the technique of controlling certainty and with well-designed control records, members of an operating group should know where they are going, where they are now, and where they wanted to go when they started the cycle of action under review.

CONTROLLING CERTAINTIES: EXPOSE CONDITIONS

C 5–1: *Disclose Sufficiencies*

One frequently met condition, often susceptible to definite disclosures, relates to the needs or supplies of something; that is, *sufficiencies*. Included within the broad meaning of sufficiency is oversufficiency, duplication, undersufficiency, deficiency, and optimum sufficiency.

Defects in certainty of conditions frequently center around these sufficiencies, whether they be insufficiencies or oversufficiencies. The question of sufficiencies of inventory for immediate and future requirements, for example, constantly confronts the executive. Adequate supplies of material or merchandise must be accessible at all times. By disclosing sufficiencies he reveals requirements, needs, and insufficiencies. This is often accomplished by comparing supplies of merchandise, facilities, people with similar operations, the current level of business activity, and the situation a year ago.

An executive is also concerned with the economy factor. Aligned with certainty is avoidance of waste, an economy factor that extends to the full scope of the enterprise. In examining operating techniques, procedures, and organizational patterns, he concerns himself with overlapping, duplication, and neglected functions. The question, "Why is it necessary?" may disclose these superfluous conditions.

C 5–2: *Criticize Controllables*

The executive should now critically examine the situation for useful conditions that are susceptible to management control without unreasonable cost, effort, or delay. These conditions are useful because they are adaptable to advancing the item.

The executive frequently finds that many exposed and identified conditions cannot be controlled or avoided. These are called *fixed conditions*. An executive who cannot discriminate between fixed and *controllable conditions* will have difficulty in producing adequate results. An executive may ask the question, "Why is production down on this unit?" A forelady may reply, "It's the kind of people we get these days." The kind of employees hired is obviously a fixed condition to the forelady. If she wishes to contribute to a solution, she should search for and criticize those conditions she can control. She should be alert to such controllable conditions as an improperly set machine, a dissatisfied employee, or the need for additional training. By studying situations revealed by such questions and answers, Williamson-Dickie executives have sharpened their ability to discriminate between fixed and controllable conditions.

The executive directs his criticism primarily toward material that is under his control, seeking opportunities for progress within the scope of his objectives. If the factual material is not susceptible to his control, he should be more cautious about building up his lack of satisfaction with it. In general people are more likely to criticize conditions outside the realm of their control. They are, no doubt, aware intuitively or consciously that they themselves do not bear the responsibility for these conditions.

Criticizing people is generally less effective than criticizing things and conditions. No matter how sensitive an executive may be to criticism of the conditions controllable by him, he must accept responsibility for them in effective executive operations.

One technique useful in exposing conditions on developmental items is alternately to construct and to criticize. Criticism is suspended when the construction of a framework of material is being emphasized. During Criticizing Controllables, however, emphasis is upon criticism. Defense of the merits of the material is suspended.

Fixed conditions rarely suggest opportunities as do controllable ones, and they should not be used to justify failure. When exposed, they should be identified as fixed conditions and waived. Preoccupation with fixed conditions often obscures controllable conditions. Necessity will sometimes motivate executives to unearth controllable conditions when on the surface all conditions are fixed. If selling prices, for example, are forced down ten per cent by economic conditions, this fixed condition indicates the need for greater effort to cut down operating expenses to maintain profitable operations.

In the fall of 1957, sales and profits at Williamson-Dickie declined substantially. The general economy in the United States suffered a commensurate decline. The management of Williamson-Dickie contended that, while the general decline was a fixed condition, the drop in sales and profits was something that they could and must do something about. A paperwork expert was engaged. This expert, after a preliminary investigation, demonstrated that between $50,000 and $70,000 a year could be saved in Williamson-Dickie's clerical procedure.

C 5–3: *Exhaust Possibilities*

A *possibility* is a significant and sometimes critical element within a state of affairs subject to executive consideration and action. Such a possibility is something that can be attained, that is subject to realization. It is a potentiality, probability, or likelihood within the situation. Contrasted to it would be a disadvantage, improbability, or desire.

The capable executive will attempt to exhaust all possibilities in order to insure completeness, an important aspect of certainty. At this stage he will carry the activity of exposure to the point of being reasonably certain he has exposed all conditions. He will take a look at the total situation to be sure that all possibilities have been exhausted. He will assure himself that everything possible, practicable, feasible, or expedient has been done—that nothing has been left out. Every point within this related set of circumstances is weighed as to its being worthy of attention and possible action by management.

A professional standard of thoroughness is required to adequately exhaust possibilities. Superficial handling or stopping before a solution is indicated may mean that advancement on the item will halt. In either case a senior executive may need to reprocess inadequacies. Complete exposure of conditions more certainly yields data for alternatives capable of advancing the solution. The executive exhausts his memory, sources of information, and the dimensions that may be projected into the situation. At this point he asks the question, "Do we have enough facts to go ahead to the next step?"

The degree to which efforts are applied to exhausting possibilities of the situation may determine whether the effort at solving a problem is a success or failure. The margin between a first and second alternative is frequently a narrow one, as is the margin of superiority between an industry leader and the second firm. Many one-mile races are won by only two or three steps, and the top executives in an organization usually attain their positions by the same small margin. When a new product is put into the line, it will be much more profitable if it becomes one of the top two or three products on the market. A product with a relative sales position in the lower half of the market, for example, does not reach enough volume to secure low production costs. Such products generally do not justify exhausting possibilities of intensive design efforts and may not produce enough gross profit to support an adequate inventory.

C 5–4: Establish Controls

Controls are devices that prevent an operation from going astray. They afford a standard of comparison or a means of verifying the results of experimentation. Too often, they are neglected in the early stages of an item's advancement. When the need for controls becomes self-evident, it may be too late for them to be established satisfactorily. For this reason, the scientist and the executive alike establish controls in the beginning stages of their operations.

Exposure of conditions is facilitated by the existence of standards of comparison that function as controls. Examples of such standards abound; they are continually involved when comparisons are made between estimates and results. Data from earlier periods are conveniently used as controls when their later need has been foreseen. Too often, an executive is forced into inadequate decisions because of his inability to verify the causes of his successes and his failures. If controls have been properly established, some of this uncertainty can be avoided. Positive benefits can usually be foreseen.

CONTROLLING CERTAINTIES: DEVELOP IDEAS

I 5–1: Assume Tentatives

If an executive cannot determine the certainty of a point with satisfaction, at this time he must choose between delaying advancement to allow time to determine certainty or moving ahead with a tentative assumption or working hypothesis. Under the proper circumstances, especially at the early stages of the undertaking, moving ahead is often preferable. He can include material in the plan which he assumes is valid, conditioned by the expectation that later operations will furnish an opportunity to determine its validity.

To assume is to believe with a relatively small degree of objective assurance, to approximate, or to accept with slight evidence points which have not been previously validated.

Many times an executive feels the urge to delay development of a solution until every point has been validated. If he consciously and deliberately recognizes the tentativeness of the material, however, it can be put in the record without undue effort. Often, 80 per cent of it will be valid. The executive must, of course, recognize this material for what it is—a provisional formulation. By releasing concern for certainty in this area, however, he can later reduce the area in which certainty now must be emphasized to the 20 per cent which is eliminated or validated.

A flexible attitude allows one to forgo this early certainty, so that a more valid certainty may later be produced through being able to reach actual experience earlier. When an executive's skill is developed in qualifying the tentativeness of the material he works with, his flexibility in executive operations is improved. He may selectively establish the tentativeness of information, sequence, arrangement, or grouping.

Presuppositions, impressions, and working hypotheses are all useful in executive operations. Certainty is thus constructively used by permitting uninhibited wishes and ideas to be nurtured for later development.

A substantial proportion of faith or optimism that an idea has possibilities is needed. A negative-minded individual who believes that "it can't be done" thus may hamper the development of ideas. Many practical ideas are incubated from visionary, impractical ideas which were permitted to survive and exist as working hypotheses.

The consideration of certainties calls for selectivity and balance, as overrefinement or striving for absolute certainties is costly in both time and effort. Striving to carry the solution as far as practicable and aiming at progress is usually more productive than aiming at perfection. Executives frequently qualify the objective certainty of their conclusions at the start of the action cycle and emphasize it at the end in an evolutionary or gradual approach. This provides for a flexibility of certainty to include new facts.

Some immature executives offer a mere assumption as a fact and do not qualify it. They are apparently more satisfied with this assumed condition than with the truth. Their purpose may be to establish a pretense to others who they believe want to keep things looking favorable. For good executive teamwork, each individual should edit his own assumptions and not throw to others the burden of editing and checking the validity of his assumptions. Prestige is gained by executives who cultivate an attitude of tentativeness and qualify the tentativeness of conclusions which are merely speculations.

I 5–2: Support Insights

By this time the executive should have some deeper insights about the undertaking. He should have a fuller understanding of the situation, but there are many new perceptions that cannot yet be accepted as true. Since the executive will be absorbed with the novelty and interest of the ideas, it is desirable to emphasize certainty at this point by supporting or substantiating these insights instead of merely defending them. Executives should search for relevant data helping to prove their belief in the validity of them.

An *insight* is a mental visualization, purporting to present a valid fact, problem, or intended action. The insight may be a mere sensed illusion or doubt; or it may, in fact, represent a reality. In order for the executive to be more certain of validity, he should endeavor to detect and recognize fallacies and false premises. His logic should be rational, and his acceptance of facts realistic.

Skillful executives go below the superficial level to support their conclusions. Immature executives sometimes think they know the answers but have no support or grounds for their beliefs. Executives need to take the responsibility for their own factual positions. When they try to prove something is correct or false, they should edit their own factual positions.

Frequently, opinions of problems may be nonvalid assumptions, because the individual giving the information has not gone to the trouble of validating or supporting his insights. The executive may ask this individual the question, "What operation in the line is causing the difficulty?" When the answer is received, he endeavors to learn if this insight has support by asking, "What are the grounds for your belief?" or "Can you give us figures to substantiate this answer?" The reporting person then should try to corroborate or correlate the tentative belief. A naked "belief" should never be accepted.

The classic answer to the question, "Why is production down on Unit X?" (before our emphasis of *Expose Conditions* as an early step) was: "First one thing and then another." Other examples of unvalidated opinions were: A preceding operator was not trimming her work, causing the operation under study to take too much time, or the r.p.m. of the machine at the bottleneck operation was below standard.

Executives, just as lawyers and judges do, should draw a sharp line of discrimination between fact and inference. They should place emphasis upon provable evidence, supported by exhibits, witnesses, and admissions. Figures as well as facts are useful in supporting insight. Support Insights is closely related to another EOT guide point, Modify Reservations.

I 5–3: *Provide Risk Margins*

Executives frequently calculate expected performance on their intentions, but past experience indicates that they should also expect omissions, miscalculations, and surprises in the future. If they go into a situation with eyes open, expecting a sure thing when they have not set up a margin of safety, they are not following a precaution frequently taken by successful executives; that is, to provide a risk margin.

Executives are not always able to arrange for statistically supported or objective assurance, so a margin of safety is usually necessary. Subjective assurance or mere intensity of belief unsupported by facts is not grounds for an unnecessary risk.

A *risk margin* must provide for the chance of loss and perils. It must take into account the degree of probability of errors in judgment. It is an anticipated extent of effort or performance over and above that ordinarily required. These safety factors or extra allowances are fundamental in executive operations.

When a risk margin is provided, it is assumed that a solution of some sort has been developed, usually by a senior executive. Frequently this solution will be adequate only if there are no unforeseen deterrents or obstacles. Furthermore, the solution is provided only up to reasonable expectations. If the efficiency of a department is only 70 per cent, for example, and the efficiency required is 90 per cent, the experienced executive may provide a solution which could conceivably result in a 100 per cent efficient department. This solution would allow a 10 per cent margin of safety.

Some solutions are accepted as being adequate which with a satisfactory risk margin would be inadequate. More potent alternatives are needed to provide this margin. It requires more work to set up predicted success with such a margin of adequate assurance.

I 5–4: Verify Accuracies

One aspect of controlling certainty is executive concern with the accuracy and validity of their operating material. Since their energies are directed toward areas of opportunity indicated by previously exposed elements of operating material, accuracy is essential. If these areas of opportunity have been inaccurately recorded or reported, they waste the executive's time and effort when he attempts to arrive at a solution.

An inaccuracy may materialize as a mistake, fallacy, or oversight. Usually it is a representation of something done or handled, such as an answer, detail, or conclusion. Accuracy is the fidelity to fact or truth, usually attained by the exercise of care. Factual accuracy is the correspondence of a statement or representation to the actual facts.

In *verifying accuracies*, executives put the operating material thus far assembled to certain tests. These tests may be mathematical, experimental, or in the form of questions to others, just so long as they serve the purpose of revealing faults and inaccuracies. Executives also apply statistical tests to indicate the soundness of their conclusions. Psychologists have developed an interesting differentiation in the validation of tests. According to one, a valid test is one which is useful or which adequately predicts the characteristics sought after. A reliable test, on the other hand, is one which consistently measures the trait in question from one test to the next.

Accuracy's importance is obvious, and there are examples of its continuing need throughout any organization. For example, if an adequate job of controlling inventory is to be done, accurate estimated and actual sales or production figures are essential. Capable executives are constantly striving to avoid developing conclusions built on inaccuracies.

CONTROLLING CERTAINTIES: UNIFY VIEWS

V 5-1: *Condition Atmosphere*

Atmosphere is seen or felt evidence of surrounding influences, pervading and affecting human relations and attitudes favorably or unfavorably. These environmental influences should be recognized and controlled if possible. Distractions, fatigue, nosie, temperature, light, air, and space are areas in which the physical atmosphere may be affected favorably or unfavorably.

For effective unification of views, executives cultivate or condition this atmosphere by adapting or modifying these influences so they will favor the intended goal. Proper environment and atmosphere influence reactions of members of a group favorably to successful cooperative efforts.

An atmosphere of factual detachment is more productive than one of personal involvement or emotional bias. When this objective attitude exists, rigidity is overcome by flexibility for a free and spontaneous interchange of views. Progress in unification is usually made when all concerned sincerely emphasize unification of views in this manner. A previously conditioned favorable climate of harmonious relations is generally more significant than the actions immediately preceding efforts at unification of views. Prestige and mutual respect are evidence of such a climate.

Responses of others depend upon personal feelings in addition to objective logic. These feelings are influenced by the atmosphere in which the proposition is discussed. If a senior is seeking the support of junior executives, he should be alert to the need for favorable attention and proper atmosphere in addition to the mere content of his statement.

Many effective unifying moves cause emotional responses more than logical reactions. An executive may use these influences to condition the listener's favorable attention and interest. Salesmen take steps to gain favor for themselves in the eyes of their prospects; executives in relations with their associates do the same thing. In sales work the salesman frequently is required to make two sales. In addition to the final sale, in the "play for showdown" he must "sell" the prospect to permit him to open his sample case and to discuss the proposition. If the buyer has willingly agreed to look at the samples, he is better conditioned to receive the presentation.

Encouragement and recognition have a positive effect in gaining favor, while discouragement and belittlement have a negative one. Sincere compliments appeal to the pride of the individual. A proposition advanced by an individual loses its momentum if it is received defensively. If the person whose acceptance and support is being sought is not in rapport, it frequently is not practicable to carry the discussion further on a purely logical or factual basis.

A well-prepared, printed, and illustrated statement which can be read in privacy is much more likely to be well received than a haphazard, oral presentation made in a noisy plant with constant interruptions.

V 5–2: *Reconcile Inconsistencies*

After factors have been integrated, inconsistencies may appear in the factors themselves or in the viewpoints of the executives regarding them. These inconsistencies need to be reconciled or resolved if others are to accept the solution as a working pattern possible of accomplishment. To *reconcile* is to make agree to, bring into correspondence, or demonstrate to one or another's satisfaction the fundamental consistency of things. *Inconsistency* is a lack of agreement or harmony, variance, or failure to hold to the same principles or course of action. It consists of being not agreeable to one another or not in agreement; that is, incompatible.

Inconsistencies in views are inevitable in a group. The logical incompatibility of viewpoints should not exclude any from consideration. The executive's job is to effect a reconciliation between them so that a conclusion can be reached. Otherwise a stalemate may stop advancement. These inconsistencies are in themselves relations. They may be listed, and the executive can decide which differences of viewpoint are most useful and which are potentially destructive. Some differences, for example, may reflect a fundamental, unresolved conflict or inconsistency of the situation. On the other hand, some differences may result from superficial reasoning or prejudice.

Ordinarily, associates are expected to be reasonable in their dealings, which does not prevent an honest difference of opinion or a constructive statement of opposition. Occasionally, however, the executive must deal with a difficult personality problem—either a chronic one or one made difficult by the immediate circumstances. At this point, an appeal to logical or factual reasoning is of little effect. The executive may need to center attention upon the position taken by the nonunified individual and seek to expose sound points in favor of the conflicting position. He can credit that position with these points and then isolate other points favorable to a more constructive solution. Then he endeavors to justify how these apparently sound points may have been misinterpreted with relation to the entire proposition. This tolerance of the opposition is more effective than returning opposition with direct opposition. Much opposition comes from fears that have not been definitely exposed or identified.

If everyone's effort is centered upon the situation and if everyone is seeking to reconcile the inconsistencies constructively and rationally, some integrated solution usually will be found. An effective type of leader participation is to recognize such issues and to sense opportunities for their resolution.

Views sometimes differ because the individuals involved do not have the same perspectives. One view may be aligned with the scope of long-time possibilities, while another may be in line with a short-time view. For the sake of effective operations, these views need to be reconciled and one common scope chosen for the immediate purpose.

The inconsistencies which the executive aims to reconcile are not necessarily differences in understanding. They may be inconsistencies in the material with which each individual is working. Two or more individuals may visualize the content of the situation differently. These factors, when viewed objectively, may be logically incompatible, and it is the function of the executive to alter them in such a way that there will be established a harmonious relationship.

In production planning the objective is to keep the plant operating to provide steady employment, to control inventory, and to fill orders promptly. On the other hand, inventory should not rise beyond the financial capacity of the company. If, for example, all the plans are made, and the inventory is 30 per cent more than the company can afford, then there is an unresolved inconsistency. Often the treasurer from his perspective will become aware of this and will point out the need to resolve this inconsistency.

Emphasis upon the reconciling of inconsistency in an organization requires a perspective focused at the full scope of the enterprise. Company-wide standardization is an example of this principle. Sometimes executives permit several inconsistent views to remain in a compromise plan designed to accommodate the views of all. This is a frequently wasteful and unsatisfactory substitute.

Some unexplained inconsistencies at a broader scope of different perspective will be consistent. An example of this is found in the EOT cycle when "results" in one cycle may become "conditions" in the next or following cycle of effort.

V 5–3: Stratify Confidences

Confidence is conviction in the certainty of an occurrence or in the correctness of an assumption. There are degrees of firmness of these convictions so it is frequently possible to break a proposition down into areas of certainty and uncertainty. The executive will be certain about some things in the proposition and will have reservations about others. As these points of confidence emerge, they may be grouped as to degrees of confidence. In this way each group is assigned a stratum or level of confidence.

It is usually possible to stratify confidences usefully. The more factors an executive is confident or certain of and can release concern on, the narrower is the area in which to intensify effort. He can thus concentrate on factors which he believes to be uncertain and in need of advancement.

An executive's own attitude may be stratified. In certain areas he may be overcautious or timid, whereas a calculated risk might be more productive. Big steps, of course, usually require more proof than small ones. Dread of the complexity or impossibility of an undertaking frequently interferes with effective action. A capable, experienced executive learns to avoid this confusion by starting early.

Confidences may be selective in terms of individuals. Some individuals are more sincere and believable than others; some offer mere "lip service." Underconfidence frequently interferes with executive operations as does overconfidence.

V 5–4: Agree on Courses

It is important that each member of a work group have confidence in the certainty or validity of a proposed course of action. One object of the Unify Views step is for all concerned to agree on such a course for the undertaking. A *course* is a possible, future direction indicated by a series of actions a situation is expected to undergo. All members of the group should agree on a single course before certainty is favorably indicated.

When a course is agreed upon, it is assumed that all major divergent issues of the course have been reconciled and that all concerned concur with the official, agreed course. Good judgment is a requisite in arriving at effective courses of action, since no techniques are available which will persuade people to accept unsound propositions consistently.

If the proposed course of action is expected to encounter difficulty, agreement before producing action reduces later criticism. It is also wasteful in executive operations for members of a group to agree outwardly on a single course of action and then to disagree after action is actually started. To prevent setting in motion alternative and sometimes conflicting courses of action, executives should make known in advance any reservations about such courses so there will be no mistake as to agreement on them. Questions such as, "Are we fully agreed on the next step?" help in exposing lack of agreement.

Some items delegated to a junior executive do not advance because the junior executive's enthusiasm for the subject may lead him to set up a somewhat different item on his own, which in effect competes for attention with the original item. An example of how "competing items" might originate developed when Williamson-Dickie established a branch plant.

We had broken down the entire undertaking into facilities, personnel, and records needed for the establishment of this branch plant. Our course was agreed on and items were set up for all three components of the plan at the operating division level. The Treasurer took responsibility for records to be developed for the branch. The survey of records needed presented opportunities for possible simplifying combinations. If the Treasurer had then launched independently an additional item for developing records over the entire company as he had considered, his item and the more limited but urgent item of the General Manager would have competed. In such event, the demands upon the time and creative thought of the responsible executives would probably have meant that neither item would have received enough effort to do them full justice.

It might be well to point out that the item *developing records for the branch plant* is centered upon the concrete situation, whereas the item *developing records in general* derives from a broad continuing objective. Both, however, were prompted by the discussion of records. The functionally responsible executive in this case independently created the second item without any prompting from the senior executive. In many cases such as this, pride of authorship in the junior's item gains for it more attention, even though as in this case the item of smaller scope was currently more crucial to the company strategy and to the current coordination needs. This is the reason for possibly considering only one item at a time in a particular area. At any rate, the priority of items is an important point for clear agreement between the junior and senior executives concerned with item advancement.

Creative initiative or expression on the part of the junior executive is always appropriate in the form of recommendations based on what he sees is needed to advance the entire undertaken item. In this way the role of the senior executive would be one of mere approval or of lending his broader perspective for the use and counsel of the junior executive.

The main caution is for a junior executive not to substitute an item in place of the situation-based item agreed upon. The problem here is to maintain the initiative of the junior executive and at the same time to make sure that the course agreed upon gets coordinated action. The specific item often has high value for breaking up a log jam blocking the progress of the company as a whole, even though it may appear of minor significance to a junior executive.

CONTROLLING CERTAINTIES: DETERMINE PLANS

P 5–1: Declare Standards

A *standard* is an expression of the results desired from any given activity, inventory, or quality. It is generally intended for representative use, and may be expressed by figures, models, or descriptions. Standards are often used as a basis of comparison and then may become formal criteria of satisfaction.

Standards may be applicable in many instances, requiring no redetermination with each individual situation. Standards are norms, specifications, or models, and are considered a kind of a plan. Informal or tentative norms may precede firm standards. Results expectations usually apply as goals in one undertaken item or project. Standards are of more general application. They generally are proven to be attainable before final adoption.

All have individual standards of satisfaction, but company standards may be shared by members of a group, as professional standards are shared by members of a profession.

Every executive knows the meaning of the word *declare*. Some executives, however, fail to follow its meaning literally in regard to standards. Standards should be put into words and stated or published with firm conviction. One of the functions of executive operations is to choose and declare standards. They should not be eased or reversed without serious consideration.

Many standards are utilized in executive operations techniques. Declaring mathematical standards is a common practice. Industrial engineers use them, for example, in setting incentive rates. Standards are less frequently used when adding new features to a product line. The Research Department at Williamson-Dickie does not introduce a new feature unless a ratio of at least 60/40 of the consumers surveyed have approved it. They are thereby assured that the proposed feature is an improvement—not a mere change.

A standard need not be mathematical; it may be descriptive. The "successful Dickie dealer" used as a criterion in the Dickie Dealer Profit Plan exemplifies a descriptive standard.

P 5–2: Eliminate Nonessentials

Nonessentials are content elements that may be removed without vitally affecting some primary or useful function. They are the unnecessaries, dispensables, irrelevants, suppositions, and presumptions usually present unless removed.

Eliminating nonessentials calls for the executive to boil down, remove, or discard. In one way or another he must waive or exclude from consideration nonessential material that impedes advancement of the item.

A versatile executive has previously worked energetically to include every relevant element for consideration. Now he must reverse his emphasis and work on non-inclusion. Because the executive seldom has time for an orderly elimination of this material, he may in one sense learn to tolerate incidentals. He isolates, defers, waives, or skips over the material which does not contribute to advancement of the undertaking.

Much nonuseful material may be included for logical consistency alone —to round out a subject. Unfortunately, some individuals have a propensity for including nonessentials which serve to slow down item advancement.

Many plans come under the heading of nonessentials, and executives need to realize their lack of value. Nonessential plans frequently result from overoptimistic ideas, or from an inadequately conceived or outgrown need.

Nonessentials thus accumulate even though there no longer is a need for them. Economic necessity often serves as the impetus to eliminate them. During the Williamson-Dickie economy drive in 1957, a consultant uncovered numerous opportunities to eliminate such nonessentials. His suggestions to eliminate overlapping and duplicated work permitted savings of $24,000 that year in the Credit Department alone.

Executives should be constantly on the alert for opportunities to eliminate nonessentials. Frequently, a production operation can be eliminated entirely by taking advantage of a pause in another operation. A Work Clothes Rental Service final inspection was eliminated in this manner. It was possible to perform this operation during the pause while a pressing operator waited for her press to take effect.

P 5–3: Anticipate Contingencies

Contingencies are possible future developments which are considered and provided for with greater than usual caution in advance. In seeking to avoid oversights, the executive endeavors to take adequate precautions and sets up safeguards with as much forethought as possible. To *anticipate* is to take a possible future event into consideration in advance of its happening and to provide for future contingencies relating to it.

Executives definitely have the responsibility for their anticipated contingencies. Foresight in anticipating these future developments is a constant concern in executive operations. Of course, there are many calculated risks that are required by the executive. He goes into these with his eyes open, so to speak. Executives should try to avoid omissions or oversights that might cause surprise and inconvenience. Careless executives later find points overlooked or not anticipated which may be key points that can make or break the undertaken item. A principal usefulness in anticipating obstacles and omissions is visual projection of the activities and subject areas with which the executive will deal. If this is done definitely, details of the plan can be expressed in writing for communication between those involved.

Adequate projection of expected future operations requires imagination, experience, and training. It involves dealing with abstract representations of possible future events and considerations which need to be handled in as positive and as definite a manner as are present and immediate realities. Frequently, clues appearing in only a small area might indicate the possibility of a major involvement. Contingencies must be anticipated early as flexibility hardens with age, and they are more difficult to alter.

Sometimes pointing out the problem will prevent the recurrence of a similar situation. In such cases the future benefit in proportion to time spent is of more value than trying to recover and patch up the old situation. The adage, "Do not cry over spilled milk" illustrates this point. Many contingencies are anticipated by writing them down, so they will serve as reminders. This is especially true in dealing with procedures where errors are repeated.

P 5-4: *Qualify Commitments*

A *commitment* is a mutual understanding between individuals, in which one individual accepts responsibility for a plan's accuracy or certainty of performance. It is a statement—offered by one executive and received by another—in which the quality of certainty is an important factor. To *qualify* is to moderate a statement, understanding, or commitment in such a way that it will represent the ultimately expected performance.

A question asking, "Is there any reason why that cannot be completed as planned?" endeavors to qualify a commitment. It is helpful to consider conditions which may be relevant or decisive in qualifying the expected outcome of a plan so they can be taken into account. Another consideration is the likelihood of the commitment's being achieved, as well as the ability and reliability of the person making it. This may lead to changing the commitment somewhat to make it more performable.

If 30 per cent of the employees in a production department are trainees, this would be legitimate grounds for qualifying a commitment made on the basis of an experienced department. Other qualifying conditions relating to the commitment might be: age in training hours, date plans were determined, per cent of rejects in production, unforeseen policy changes, number of hours worked during week, and absentees after a holiday.

It is also a worthwhile precaution for an executive to qualify the acceptance of an unreasonable or nonperformable assignment made to him. This does not mean, however, he is to attempt to reduce the assignments and duties that are normally expected of him.

Certainty is an important consideration, and when an executive gives a commitment, it should not be given or taken lightly. From the other extreme, however, only an immature executive will expect action merely because someone has promised to do it. The statements, "You promised . . ." and "You told me . . ." are generally nonuseful executive rejoinders following an inadequate performance. The mature executive in such a case evaluates the reliability of the executive making such commitments and is guided accordingly in future dealings.

A promise is sometimes not considered to be a commitment by the person who makes it, but the beneficiary is likely to view it as a commitment. At this point the essential qualification of character is displayed, and rash promises or "lip service" are just as unsatisfactory as expressed nonacceptance of a responsibility.

CONTROLLING CERTAINTIES: PRODUCE ACTIONS

A 5–1: Intensify Determinations

Producing action calls for effort sufficient to move the item forward. Broadly, it is the act of causing occurrences that will influence a situation to advance toward a desired result.

Much of the time a good start is the only action needed to advance an item. If a sufficiently substantial margin of certainty has been set up, the immediate objective will be energetically accomplished. When efforts have declined, however, determination must be intensified to maintain action and advancement.

Determination is the impulse that drives an individual to action for results. It permits continuous, intensive advancement efforts upon the undertaken item. This resolution or staying power is a vital ingredient in executive operations.

Determination is essential to achievement. Drive, energy, and tenacity develop the power to get things done. When an executive senses that the undertaken item is not advancing toward a conclusion, he needs to intensify his emphasis to maintain continuity of effort. To *intensify* is to deepen or strengthen impelling forces, such as resolution or concentration upon a purpose.

When an executive is "on top" of details, his intense effort is likely to be productive. When he is submerged in details and under pressure, the result may be frustration and worry.

Sometimes, anger or fear can generate the necessary intensity of determination. A more positive determination is based upon a will to succeed in the undertaking.

An ineffective, negative individual, or one who is reconciled to failure usually lacks that measure of effort necessary for success. He stalls action on the item until an effective executive supplies the necessary determination. Such a weak-willed individual is likely to retard action in all functions under his responsibility.

By maneuvering the forces and conditions, the determined executive is able to apply his effort at the best time. In other words, he can "strike while the iron is hot."

In 1957, business decline and competition intensified determination of Williamson-Dickie's management to reduce costs. One executive who was aware of Williamson-Dickie's 35-year effort to reduce costs commented, "You can't get blood out of a turnip." Nevertheless in 1959, the General Manager tabulated results of the intensified drive to reduce costs. Estimated savings were as follows:

2% Maximum Shrinkage on Cloth vs. "Sanforized"—$100,000.

Extra discount secured from suppliers—$250,000.

Expense reduction through budgeting—$50,000.

These items saved $400,000 a year. Gross profit increase due to an improvement in designing added another $200,000. Intensified determinations effected a total annual savings of $600,000.

A 5–2: Emphasize Advancements

Stationary items often are reactivated at the Intensify Determinations step. Care must be exercised, however, that determination is directed toward advancements. *Advancement* is any change or operation that materializes in a move forward along the path toward results. It means completing a forward movement however small. The high intensity of determination needed at this point is seldom built up on a team basis, as only one or two individuals will get "mad" at the item. Executives can usually secure group cooperation toward advancement.

Frequently item advancement loses ground because every member of the team does not stress it. Other activities dilute emphasis on advancement. The executive should carefully gauge his emphasis so that he pushes important items hardest.

The inclination of certain executives to set up competing items has already been discussed. When a competing item is undertaken, it typically diverts effort from the central objective.

The executive is expected to contribute advancement efforts and energy—not inertia, resistance, noncooperation, or de-emphasis. One or two indifferent individuals may quibble about the situation, neutralizing valuable advancement time and energy.

Unnecessary worry or concern over minor imperfections and irritations must be set aside so that the main emphasis can be placed on producing results. Even though the final action which produces completion sometimes may seem remote, the executive must be generally aware of the objective. More immediate handling of steps in an item's advancement also produces progress toward a completed goal. Because these daily activities are almost a constant concern, care must be taken that both immediate and remote actions are emphasized.

A 5–3: *Account for Modifications*

When any cycle of action is completed, the result will not be identical with what was previously visualized. There will be modifications resulting from developments which did not materialize exactly as expected. *Modifications* are partial changes in form or quality of an objective. They affect the alignment of results with the central objective and may restrict the full realization as previously intended or visualized.

In examining modifications, the executive must be familiar with the conformities, observances, or correspondences with the desired plan. In this he aims to reckon with the completed undertaking in order to decide and explain its acceptability. He needs to justify, reconcile, or bear out the validity of the modifications.

The main thing to consider at this point is that these materialized modifications should be accounted for. If they are the result of the responsible executive's failure to center on the end result, they are within his control and responsibility. If they were not necessary or justified and if they reduce or dilute the central objective, then the executive has not kept faith with the objective of the management team.

A 5–4: *Test Completions*

A *completion* is the final form of an undertaking after realization. A completion is the fulfillment, finish, or consummation of executive efforts. It needs to be tested to be sure that incompletions, nonperformances, or abandonments have not been mistaken for valid completions.

To *test* is to submit an assumption or conclusion to a process by which it is proved true or false; that is, to prove or verify. The executive is not following the reminder to test completions if he endeavors to assume completion or excuse incompletion. Testing completions is a certainty factor that is frequently and usefully considered in executive operations. The question, "Is there anything left yet to do?" tests a completion.

The start of an undertaking or a cycle of action is surrounded by a different atmosphere from that of its finish. The start is a novel, new experience, and the obstacles and unforeseen developments do not appear as formidable as they do well along the road to completion. Some executives are better starters than finishers. In general, many more items are started than are completed. This is why executives at this point should emphasize finishing as opposed to starting.

If a junior executive does not test his own completions, it must be done by a senior executive. There are frequent cases in which a senior executive does not test completions because he has the apparently justified assumption that the executive responsible for the function involved has completed his assignment. If his decision not to test completion is later shown to be in error, then the senior executive (in the following example, the Sales Manager) is responsible for the oversight by his staff members. The following case illustrates a nontested completion:

On May 25, the General Manager of Williamson-Dickie was in New York visiting the officials of a large oil company to interchange ideas on executive development. During the visit, one of the oil company officials wanted to examine samples of Dickie garments so he could approve a pilot test of uniforms. The General Manager duly noted this request in his chronological note file. Upon returning to the office, the General Manager reported among the events of the New York trip the need for this particular set of samples to be shipped immediately. The Sales Manager and the sales staff official who was in charge of the pilot uniform service project were present at the meeting. The General Manager, of course, did not make out the order or specify the lot number, size, and other details.

Two weeks after this meeting the General Manager asked the Sales Manager if the samples were shipped in good order. It developed that no action had been taken, either by the sales staff members or the Sales Manager, and that no completion check or follow-up was evident. Although reminded that no definite assignment was given, the General Manager felt that writing all of the pilot project's orders was the function of the Sales Department staff member. By following established channels of responsibility, no assignment was necessary. Communication, however, was called for in this particular case.

This unanticipated oversight caused no loss to the company, but the executive development opportunities presented by the case were used to turn an apparent disadvantage into an advantage. The executive operating techniques involved in this particular case, especially Test Completions, were discussed quite freely by those involved.

CONTROLLING CERTAINTIES: REVIEW RESULTS

R 5–1: *Preserve Experiences*

Experiences are any operations which have been observed, completed, or lived through. They are participations, proceedings, or personal knowledge. Theoretical knowledge, inexperience, or future destiny cannot substitute for experience and the knowledge gained and preserved from it.

Each cycle of an item advancement involves expenditure of considerable effort and the exercise of the maximum skill then in possession of the executive or executive group. Every experience the group passes through should yield a certain increment of skill which may be used in the future. If possible these favorable and unfavorable experiences, instead of being merely personal, should be available to others interested in similar situations. Abstractions from particular experiences are sometimes difficult to recall. Therefore, it is desirable to preserve the histories of experiences so the material and skills may be used again. Preserved in accessible form they permit the tie-in of different advancement efforts of one item or objective in depth of time.

To *preserve* is to fix or to put something away in such form and place that it will continue to be available for reuse; in other words, to retain, save, or keep, as contrasted to, to lose, abandon, or forget. The value of experiences is greatly amplified when preserved for company or broader use.

Experience records are preserved in Williamson-Dickie files in the most convenient form under the circumstances. These records may be in narrative form—as in a progress report—or they may consist of descriptive accumulations or check lists of typical reminders. A check list would ordinarily be an alphabetical listing, or possibly sequenced numerically. The experience record may also consist of figures, preserving inventory experience at a certain time, or the activity during a certain period. The material should be condensed without sacrificing its value as reminder or reference to particular details.

The need for reference to past experience arises frequently. During World War II, the shortages of manpower were more critical than at present, and recruiting efforts were much more intensive. The experience records of alternatives used to recruit personnel during World War II are preserved at Williamson-Dickie and can be used as reminders.

The growing executive makes use of experience as a part of the permanent make-up of his body of skills. Experience helps make the most of the three characteristics of executive success—intelligence, character, and drive—which have been discussed previously. Each executive has preserved ten, twenty, or possibly thirty or more years of experience in his own person.

The number of years of exposure to experience does not necessarily mean that all executives acquire the same amount of experience in the same number of years. At one time, Williamson-Dickie placed considerable emphasis on garment industry experience in selecting and employing salesmen. A vocabulary test was developed of textile-garment terminology which revealed how much knowledge of his industry an individual had picked up in five, ten, or possibly twenty years of company experience. It is disappointing to find men available for employment who, although they have been in the industry as long as 15 years, still cannot speak the trade language.

R 5–2: *Carry Over Knowns*

Each experience in addition to the objective results produced, is useful in its own account and should be preserved for utilization in later cycles. These experiences are especially useful when it is necessary to reprocess the same or a related item. When the executive carries over knowns, he emphasizes an evolutionary building-on approach as well as a revolutionary reconstruction approach.

Things known from experiences range from useful particulars to helpful generalizations. Utilizing these known content elements from experience of the previous cycle amplifies background and speeds preliminaries. The executive, for example, will not need to repeat previously handled operations. Generalizations such as break down schemes can be used again in the new cycle. Exposed conditions are also knowns which can be carried over.

Some of these knowns may be available from memory, while others may require reference to past notes. All notes, therefore, need to be preserved, indexed, and possibly reproduced, so that their useful content elements will serve as material for the next effort.

The reference condition of information has a substantial effect upon its convenience and continuity. The integrity and convenience of reference books and files affect the ability of the executive group to carry over known information to future item advancement efforts.

R 5-3: *Survey Consequences*

All the previous steps in the cycle—essential though they may be to a successful conclusion—are subordinated in this review step to satisfactory, checked-out consequences. The executive is now ready to take a broad look at these consequences. This is his last look at the situation as it applies to the cycle just completed.

In *surveying consequences*, the executive withdraws and takes a larger view of the situation—a post-mortem examination or critique. In reflecting upon certainty at this point, he examines final results of the entire situation at the full scope. He recapitulates or digests advancement with the advantage of being able to survey the full scope in addition to having available its broken down and arranged parts. He examines the consequences of the cycle of effort with relation to the requirements of the situations. He checks what has transpired with the broad continuing objective and the immediate need. In the early stages of determining plans, he viewed the operation in prospect. The executive's purpose at this guide point is to take a look at the operation in retrospect.

Consequences that are surveyed in retrospect are not necessarily the results previously planned. For example, if all-out energy has not been applied by everyone concerned, the advancement effort cannot be expected to yield encouraging consequences. Improperly conceived undertakings will not yield satisfactory results in any event.

R 5-4: *Acknowledge Realities*

Realities are steps or intentions which have been completed or achieved. They are substantive, realized events or situations. They are not mere outward appearances or forms. Instead they are true and undistorted representations of what has actually happened. In reviewing results, the executive involved must acknowledge, recognize, or admit the existence or truth of these realities. He must concede, admit, or grant them and not attempt to justify unsatisfactory results exposed.

To attain the objectivity needed for acknowledging realities, the executive should strive to set aside self-consciousness. He should review the events disclosed completely apart from his own personal feelings, reflections, or personal prejudice. This review should be realistic rather than rationalistic. Even though the hope or intention of a successful result has been so strong that review may be colored by wishful thinking, the executive must not disown or cover up the reality of an unfavorable performance.

Prolonged minor errors which have not been acknowledged can sometimes assume major proportions. Much time and effort can be saved if each executive frankly admits his mistakes as soon as he discovers them. Some immature individuals think they lose prestige when they reverse their positions in this manner. They keep silent on their errors until the inevitable adjustment comes. Executives are more likely to be given credit for being objective and open-minded if they quickly acknowledge errors. In this way corrective action is used as an advantage in the situation and to the personal prestige of the executive.

Executives' lack of satisfaction with results may diminish if non-accomplishment continues. They tend to get immune to poor results or no results. For example, Lot 252 indicated a shelf stock of 1.2 weeks' supply, when the minimum standard is 4.0 weeks' supply. After seeing this unsatisfactory figure week after week for several weeks, an executive may become complacent. But long distance telephone calls reporting many customer complaints can shock him out of his complacency. Actions will indicate that he has acknowledged realities with the aid of external pressures and intervention. All executives need to generate this realistic view from within; in other words, they must acknowledge and face their own accomplishments.

Questions such as the following help emphasize the adequacy of our accomplishments:

Have we wasted our time?

What have we accomplished?

Is there any individual commitment related to the previously set plan?

The level of performance at which an executive is satisfied becomes the final consideration in management. Many have held that the ultimate function of the executive is control of risks. Help can be secured in estimating them. Determining the standards to be met, however, cannot be delegated. The ultimate consideration, therefore, is evaluating satisfaction.

IX

Evaluating Satisfactions

Satisfaction is a tangible response by an individual to a situation or to an aspect of a situation. Satisfactions and views both deal with feelings and personal responses of individuals. Views indicate preference and thus may be more directional in nature. Satisfaction indicates intensity of feeling. This intensity has a basis of factual and logical consistency; it is more than mere emotional stimulus and response. Although many people evaluate by imitation, intelligent satisfaction has a more valid basis of motivation.

Satisfaction may involve degrees of appreciation, starting with attention and ranging through interest, concern, and emphasis. Many people never get adequate results because they are too easily satisfied with conditions confronting them. Consistent awareness of satisfaction over a period of years may be both a cause and a result of effective operations, and is somewhat akin to time awareness.

The executive's response at this point should lean toward a lack of complete satisfaction with the situation. A high threshold of satisfaction need not cause the executive to become frustrated nor should it cause other executives to be resentful. Properly balanced attitudes of satisfaction develop a constructive sense of urgency. This sense of urgency should be in keeping with the ability to handle items within the standards set by an individual. A perfectionist's standards are desirable if counterbalanced by an objective attitude and an adequate operating technique.

When an executive senses the urgency of a need, his response to a satisfaction standard is evident. That which he tolerates may well be reviewed periodically, so he can determine if he is "satisfied" merely because something is difficult to correct. Nature builds her own protective covering over irritants, and the executive must evaluate satisfaction frequently so that he will not lose his sensitivity to facts. A consistently high standard of satisfaction is a valuable executive asset.

Individual standards of satisfaction differ between particular areas. Satisfaction may thus be applied selectively. A standard of satisfaction is more useful when considered objectively in relation to the external situation. A self-starting executive responds aggressively but objectively to conditions in situations. This objectivity can be tested by comparison with the satisfaction of others. Sometimes definite performance standards are available, and the measured results at which an executive aims make up a satisfaction standard.

The value of results, conditions, ideas, plans, or actions is based upon their real or supposed worth, usefulness, or importance. Evaluation implies a choice between two or more alternatives. Choosing between only two alternatives is relatively easy, but evaluating becomes more difficult as the number of alternatives increases. At this point a decision is needed as to the exclusion or inclusion of the alternatives being evaluated, which in itself calls for evaluation. Absolute evaluation is hardly attainable, so executive operations deal almost exclusively with relative evaluation.

Evaluation nearly always has a basis that may be traced back to how well any action or element of operating material satisfies a purpose. Frequently there are multiple purposes to be satisfied.

One must guard against abuse of the evaluating technique. Properly used it balances firmness with reasonableness. Executives frequently evaluate too early in the operating cycle of item advancement which excludes some useful conditions that may later upset premature ideas, views, or plans. For this reason it is wise to identify, expose, develop, and express before evaluating. In this way evaluation is suspended until it is more timely.

C 6–1: *Sense Defects*

To become skillful in exposure of conditions, an executive must possess a sensitive awareness to the peculiarities of operating situations. Sharpness of discrimination increases as he raises the level at which he becomes satisfied with the situation itself.

A critical view is to be encouraged at this step. Being critical does not necessarily mean being critical of others. That attitude defeats the purpose of exposing by putting others on the defensive to the extent that they may withhold information. All those concerned should be critically observant, concentrating on the situation's defects in order to expose information that will complete the exposure step.

For operating convenience, satisfaction must be reduced to definite entities. Dislikes, complaints, and worries concerning a situation may reveal defects. The executive is beginning to expose these defects when he asks "In what respect are you not satisfied?" Suggestions to improve the situation frequently originate from such units of satisfaction.

The elements of material appearing within a current situation call forth varying satisfaction responses from the executive. From them he senses defects or problems that may become operating opportunities. He aggressively searches for these restrictions or obstacles in order to remove them so that the item will advance.

Awareness of satisfaction with opportunities varies among individual executives. The best ideas often arise from someone else's lack of satisfaction with defects unnoticed by the individual most familiar with the conditions. Each individual possesses a satisfaction "boiling point." This may be low or volatile on certain types of controllable conditions and higher or less volatile on fixed conditions. If one executive senses defects or feels a lack of satisfaction with a situation or performance, his feeling may not be automatically shared by others. In a teamwork operation, however, each executive involved in a situation should share a similar sense of unsatisfaction after an objective evaluation.

The more effective executive immediately responds to defects in a situation and does not necessarily require detailed assignments or personal pressure. If a solution is expected, someone must generate awareness of opportunities revealed by the sensed defect. This awareness may be revealed by the question, "How well are you satisfied with this situation?"

Defects sometimes are not sensed immediately, as was the case in a label changing procedure. In January, 1955, Williamson-Dickie purchased another work clothing business. Although the volume of the new business was only seven per cent as large as Williamson-Dickie's, virtually every function and facility was duplicated. In the process of bringing together the sections of the two operations most susceptible to integration, certain products could be standardized except for superficial features. For example, integrating the production facilities by making greater use of specialized and continuous production on certain makes cut manufacturing costs substantially.

Brands and labels of the purchased business would continue to be used in marketing despite the integration of production facilities. Garments would be identical except for the label. Two alternative procedures for label identification were proposed:

(1) Production orders for both parent and subsidiary companies would be combined, but no labels (other than style and size identification) would be attached to those garments destined for the subsidiary. The smaller company could then maintain stock in its own warehouse and attach its own labels as orders were filled. If the stock turned slowly or became unbalanced in size, garments could be sent to the parent warehouse, and parent labels could be attached. Cost was estimated at ½% of net sales of the subsidiary's merchandise.

(2) Production orders would be combined, but parent labels would be attached to all garments. As the smaller firm required stock, labels would be ripped off and the smaller firm's labels substituted. Cost was estimated at three per cent of net sales on merchandise handled in this way.

Views were unified on the apparently less costly procedure, and no one sensed defects in carrying out the procedure. When put into effect, however, unforeseen difficulties arose in the production control department. Already working at capacity for the rush reason, schedulers found themselves unable to keep up with the calculations required to combine the smaller production orders from the subsidiary with those from the parent sales department. The procedure was then amended to provide that the smaller firm would receive all its orders from the parent warehouse during the rush season, labels would be ripped off, and new labels would be sewn in. Once rush season ended, production orders could be combined and label-ripping could be eliminated.

The pressure of rush business thus exposed certain defects which had not been taken into consideration in evaluating the decision to adopt the less-costly labeling procedure.

C 6-2: Select Opportunities

The activity of Exposing Conditions includes revealing helpful opportunities to advance the item. In selecting opportunities, the executive should attach sufficient importance to opportunities that may be later considered for use. Opportunities permit actions which, if taken, should produce favorable results. They are the material that ideas are built upon.

Opportunities are best exposed when the executive looks forward to solving the enlarging problem rather than when he looks backward to the receding situation. He needs to select areas of opportunity which may permit the situation to advance. For example, 30 elements of operating material obviously are too many to deal with readily. In a selective approach, he asks himself, "Which are the six or eight most useful areas of opportunity?" Thus he reduces the alternatives to a manageable number of specific but important possibilities.

It is especially important that exposure be carried to a terminal cause or condition. The opportunities suggested by such conditions then can be reported to others involved.

Sometimes, even though the executive previously has been satisfied with a situation, the urgency and necessity of a crisis may force attention upon opportunities. Sometimes external influences brought about by the government, financial sources, or labor organizations are the origin of these crises.

C 6-3: Summarize Situations

The executive should avoid a premature diagnosis of any situation. This is because the operating detail which brings the situation to his attention often is only a symptom suggesting that the entire situation needs further investigation.

Just as a doctor summarizes a medical situation when he makes a diagnosis, the executive must bring together and present briefly a situation's main issues and the key topics exposed. His diagnosis is a shortened, complete statement, summarizing his findings within that broad situation.

The situation an executive is summarizing is a significant and sometimes critical state of affairs that has been subjected to the executive's consideration. There is a definite distinction between a situation and an item. A *situation* is a body of operating material containing opportunities which, when identified by the executive, may stimulate him to action. On the other hand, an *item* is the undertaking he starts into action, prompted by an opportunity existing in the situation. The situation is an issue not yet completely explored.

The executive must now endeavor to condense or abridge the full content to permit an easier visualization of the findings of the entire effort at this point. He can also use this complete, integrated statement of the entire situation as a level of perspective to check certainty.

C 6–4: Attack Key Issues

The purpose of exposing conditions is to expose influences of success or failure upon an expected action, and the executive must be certain that he has emphasized the key elements in the situation.

The executive at this point has looked at the situation in its entirety as well as at its component parts. His analysis and evaluation has probably indicated several levels of importance that should be assigned to various information elements. Here he shifts the scope of focal emphasis from the full item to a given issue in order to apply all his energies and techniques to the narrower area before passing on to another area of coordinate rank. He must select from the problems the few which are most important because of their usefulness or urgency. For example, from 18 content elements, he will select the six forming the top strata. This smaller number of elements will then become key issues of the situation he will work upon.

Key issues should be the most consequential content elements appearing in the situation. They are areas of greatest opportunity which should open the gate to advancement of the undertaking. If an executive drops key issues in favor of a "bright idea," he almost invariably loses time and effort. Later developments may indicate whether key issues were adequately selected.

EVALUATING SATISFACTIONS: DEVELOP IDEAS

I 6–1: Simplify by Reduction

Developing, which is a critical point in the advancement cycle, many times is impossible because ideas have not been reduced to a performable status. Furthermore, ideas may apply to subject areas of different scope levels, and it will be necessary to reduce the focal scope of a situation to the area of greatest opportunity.

The mass of material confronting the executive must be reduced to a scope narrow enough for suitable action. *Reduction* is elimination or compression that lessens the complexity or number of relationships. It also brings the material into alignment with the time available to personnel concerned with action. This in turn leads to determination of a plan of action on the item consistent with available time. Reduction is a key activity in successful item advancement efforts.

Simplification is closely allied with the number of interdependent parts of a pattern. If the executive reduces the number, he simplifies. Singleness thus is a factor in consideration and action. Visualizing one strict pattern permits more intensive concentration and development. The executive sometimes must expend considerable effort, however, to reduce material down to a single status. Reducing figures to an average is an example of simplification.

Another method of simplifying by reduction is to isolate and remove separable and independent factors without affecting the central objective of the item. Another is accomplished by rearrangements or combinations that will reduce the number of parts in the situation. Combining single units which have operated in isolation into a single, central location is another example of simplifying by reduction. Centralization simplifies not only by reducing the number of locations, but also by reducing the number of people and operations involved. Combining two different makes into one make that combines the best features of each is another example.

One obvious reduction step is to select for attention and action a part rather than a whole activity. Parts which were previously analyzed as a whole are again evaluated. In analyzing a whole, opportunities may appear for combining elements that were not useful when separated. This is a common instance of creative reduction.

Any situation is usually susceptible to simplification along certain dimensions. The EOT Chart suggests points that may be used to reduce subjects. The immediate purpose of identifying a subject may be to fully understand it. Getting down to concrete particulars is beneficial. For example, precise and adequate expression eliminates unnecessary wording. Referring to the same item by several different names generally indicates an opportunity to simplify. In this case, several terms should be reduced to one representative term to identify the item.

Until the item itself has been reduced to a suitable "next step," there may be no rational basis for determining a plan of action. It must be reduced to an assignment status or to such definiteness that the next step becomes one of action. The reduction of the situation to an assignment status must be accomplished more rapidly in executive operations than in laboratory or academic work. The skill of getting quickly to the heart of the matter is developed by executives after many years of experience.

In simplifying, executives frequently arrive at patterns called *reduction schemes*. A reduction scheme differs from a breakdown scheme although both are closely related. In a breakdown scheme, the elements are of coordinate rank, as *spring, summer, autumn,* and *winter*. In a reduction scheme, the elements are of ordinate or unequal rank, as in *year, quarter, month, week,* and *day*.

Reduction schemes, or parts of them, may be used recurrently by executives within the same organization. Listing the reduction schemes customarily used in a business organization encourages awareness of the differing levels of scopes. The basis for reduction and expansion of focal scope is usually evident in the title and content of each reduction scheme.

A reduction scheme of figures might contain these elements: (1) Grand Total, (2) Total, (3) Subtotal, (4) Extension, (5) Amount per Unit, and (6) Unit.

A "Management Level Reduction Scheme" reduces the levels of management as follows:

1. Administrative Managership (as illustrated by the General Managership).
2. Operating Division Managership (Sales, Factory, and Financial Managerships as well as the Personnel Directorate).
3. Department Managership (those levels reporting to the Operating Division Managers; for instance, the Sales Manager has reporting to him: Advertising, Field Sales Managers, etc.).
4. Group Supervisorate (Production Group Supervisors or Division Sales Managers, for example).
5. Foremanship or Foreladyship (the terminal responsibility center).

Many reduction schemes have a gradient characteristic. The gradient scheme is not stratified either vertically or horizontally, but, instead, in terms of developmental or time progression. These differ from the reduction schemes already illustrated because scope is not the controlling factor.

The scheme we call "Procedural Firmness Reduction Scheme," has a gradient characteristic. It starts with (1) Standard Practice, (2) Necessary, (3) Do if Practical, (4) Recommended but Optional, and (5) Purely Optional. Discrimination between the elements is based on firmness. Let us look at another one, "Marketing Stages": (1) Consumer, (2) Dealer, (3) Salesman, (4) Factory, and (5) Source. In another frequently used scheme, the dimensions range from Development at the top to Routine at the bottom. Between these two extremes are the "Operating Development Levels" of Education, Preparation, and Execution.

I 6–2: Shift Scopes

As discussed under Circumscribe Inclusions, executives circumscribe an area of inclusion to consider. In this way they set a scope for the frame of reference surrounding the visualized areas. *Scope* may be defined as the extent of inclusion within a visualized activity or subject, and is synonymous to context, generality level, or breadth of view. Opposites might be intensity, or degree. The concept of "scope" is frequently evident in executive operations.

Executives deal continually with subjects of varying scope and also with the varying scope levels within the same subject. The ability to shift between broad and narrow scopes of reference is a desirable executive skill. In shifting from a monthly period to a weekly period, for example, the executive changes the time scope. Shifting scopes is similar to a change of subject, except that the change is in the scope of inclusion rather than in the nature of the topic. When attention is reduced to the more immediate needs, concern for the previously emphasized broader scope is released. The executive thus shifts down to a narrow scope.

The "full scope" has no subdividing categories, and the level of detail is the most general. One approach the executive may use is to start with this full scope and work down to a narrower scope. For example, "What were the total units sold last week by the entire company?" The executive first starts with the total in a synoptic perspective. Then he follows the chain of topical progression frequently effective in results-review conferences. He follows reduction schemes as to period (year, quarter, month, and week). In this way he progresses through the full situation always with an awareness of his position in time perspective and topical scope.

Several years ago, Williamson-Dickie's president spent two days in a company warehouse. The volume of shipments at this warehouse was below normal, even though both orders and merchandise were available. Their problem appeared to be insufficient production in their Shipping Department. The current records of units shipped were being kept on a weekly basis, but to expose present difficulties, these records were first reduced to a daily basis and then to an hourly basis. The purpose was to see if the steps taken to raise the shipping production to a satisfactory level would, in fact, accomplish that result.

The following questions asked by the General Manager illustrate shifting scope toward generality. If he asks the Manufacturing Superintendent, "How is the direct labor variance getting along?" a customary reply might be, "Well, Plant 1 is improving," or "Plant 5 is improving." When he asks, "I mean, how is the total variance progressing?" then he is bringing about expansion of scope or "raising the umbrella."

Ideas may arise while experimenting with widening or narrowing of the scope. In helping design an improved overall, a product development consultant pointed out that coveralls, matching pants-and-shirt sets, and overalls all satisfy the same basic need of the consumer. The first-named garments were then included in the design survey, thus broadening the scope.

A few years ago an item involving scope was designated "Direct Labor Cost Control." This title was too general in scope for the operating superintendent who had scheduled it. Having neither start nor stop, it appeared to be a broad, continuing objective. The next step set up for this item, "Develop Method for Using Line Improvement Procedure in Branch Plants," was actually of item scope at the superintendent's level. "Select Problem Operation for Plant 3" seemed sufficiently narrow in scope to gain immediate action status, and it became the next step.

Sometimes in developing ideas the scope can be helpfully reduced to one of several subdividing categories of the full scope. For example, if one-fourth of the direct labor variance is concentrated in one of nine plants, narrowing the scope to one-ninth will intensify the force and leverage of effort to this one plant.

In all the schemes representing differences in scope lies a useful paradox: *narrowing permits expansion*. For instance, an analyst may narrow the physical reference from a general level of the United States as a market area to the specific level of one territory, or from a general level of total production to the specific level of one bundle of processed work. Reducing this physical reference to one territory and studying one particular case generally permits broader and more detailed observation. This reduction permits expansion to a wider range of consideration or a full cycle of process steps. Conversely, selecting one consideration permits useful application of that factor to a number of physical units throughout the organization.

Fitting together content elements of different scopes suggests an hourglass pattern for the advancement cycle. For example, in observing a situation, the first perspective may be the full scope. There is no apparent order at this point. There is no visualization of composition or the interrelation of parts. The scope of reference may be reduced to a narrower level when the content elements are exposed and studied one by one in series. When completely assembled, the elements may be arranged so as to permit a reduced focal perspective. Thus the composition elements of the subject's full scope may be dealt with individually at the narrower reduced level. After arranging the composite elements, the broader scope levels may be built up. Finally, the elements can be structured into the pattern equal to the subject's full scope to complete the end of the hourglass pattern.

Even though both ends of the hourglass pattern represent the full scope, the ends differ in that the first view involves no organization of content, whereas the final representation implies an organized pattern. For this reason, the pattern developed from experience with one pilot unit may be multiplied by general application to a greater quantity of units.

The importance of scope selection, both for operating results and for executive development, becomes clear after watching the experience of a considerable number of executives. Some executives customarily select scopes that are too broad while others select scopes that are too narrow. This selection of scope for attention is influenced all too often more by the unconscious perspective of the individual than by the merits of his situation.

The length of the time period usually dealt with is related to the executive's level in the organization. Generally, the higher the executive's organizational level, the longer is the time span he takes into account. In operating situations, and especially those viewed at a supervisory level close to the actual production, shorter periods such as the month, week, day, and hour may be more suitable.

Scope can be applied to managing an executive career. Each individual executive has his own objectives and aspirations, the fulfillment of which is measured by his accomplishments during the time period involved. Inconclusive activity during a career does not tangibly fill its time span. The full scope which is most easily visualized is represented by the active career of an individual. This time scope may be too broad to be conveniently manageable, however. Executives, therefore, reduce the scope of time considerations to a more manageable period. A year has been found to be a convenient time scope for determining medium-range plans and for reviewing results.

I 6–3: Modify Reservations

At this stage of development, the executive usually has developed a number of ideas. Some of them are suitable to advancement of the item. He may feel, however, that certain features still may need improving. These doubtful features may be called *reservations*, although they do not necessarily mean the executive has no faith in the over-all item objective.

Of course, the executive should withhold evaluation until a substantial amount of material has been assembled upon which to base a valid evaluation. Nevertheless, he still may begin forming tentative conclusions of doubt or approval early in his consideration of a situation.

These reservations are similar to the defects sensed or insufficiencies disclosed earlier, except that reservations generally apply to possible alternatives. To use these preliminary reservations constructively rather than destructively, they should be used to advance the item. The executive should consider their tentative nature and indicate that he stands ready to re-examine, reappraise, and modify them as soon as more material is exposed.

The executive tries to modify these doubts or tentative uncertainties so as to avoid lack of satisfaction if the material is worthy of it. He makes sure that his reservations are objectively supported and that they are not merely subjective views. Sometimes reservations can be modified by successful pilot experiments. Expert opinions of others may dispel the executive's tentative doubts. When these reservations have been tempered or modified, the item can be released for further development.

I 6–4: Face Present Needs

In order to keep the item moving forward, the executive must concentrate upon the time-consuming but productive job of dealing with present needs. *Present needs* are conditions requiring immediate attention if an intended undertaking is to advance or if a current situation is to be kept from deteriorating.

When the executive is confronted with these exigencies, he must give realistic and balanced attention to them rather than try to evade them. Much of the time these present needs are exposed unexpectedly and without warning. Also, in handling undertaken items, he also finds that the start frequently is different from that anticipated. The immediate needs sometimes have not been previously disclosed or even thought of and may consist of small details not difficult to handle but still necessary before larger steps are taken.

Frequently an executive is so preoccupied and intent upon accomplishing an end-result that he does not consider what needs to be done now to start the item in the right direction. Present needs not connected with the project may arise. When this happens, the executive must suspend other efforts and face them.

EVALUATING SATISFACTIONS: UNIFY VIEWS

V 6–1: Appraise Tolerations

Tolerance is normally assumed to be a desirable trait, especially helpful in dealing with people. *Toleration* has a slightly different connotation. In EOT, it exists when the executive is aware of needs but endures them without attempting to take corrective action. Willingness to permit these conditions and to make allowances for them is usually disclosed when the executive determines the cost of not taking action. As tolerations are closely related to satisfactions, executives should deal constructively with both for effective operating results.

Fixed conditions frequently need to be accepted, waived, and tolerated. When appraising tolerations, however, the executive must determine how much it costs to permit apparently fixed conditions to continue. He must then set a breaking point as to when costs of inadequate performance can be tolerated no longer. The executive's role, his authority, and his responsibility, as well as other pressing items on his schedule, influence the extent to which he will permit an unsatisfactory situation to continue.

A high overhead expense of doing business, for example, may be tolerated because it is difficult to reduce. But when an aggressive competitor finds ways and means to reduce his overhead expense, the executive may abandon his complacency. Finding the cost of tolerations is a productive area where two or more executives may unify views. Each executive should examine the various areas by cost and worth to make the necessary allowances.

V 6–2: *Respond to Probable Effects*

Skilled executives usually develop conditioned responses to the stimuli of facts and satisfactions. They respond aggressively to foreseen probabilities. Inexperienced executives, on the other hand, sometimes fail to consider the relationship of cause and effect in evaluating.

Probable effects are eventual happenings indicated by the present situation. They are possible consequences which may reasonably be expected. These probable effects become influences which, if they are not responded to, may appear to be defects in evaluating.

The executive is not responding to a probable effect when he fails to plan ahead to make available an adequate number of trainers. In a period of expansion, inexperienced employees must be selected and trained for new production lines. If these trainees do not have the attention of qualified trainers, the probable effects are abnormally long training periods, subnormal productive efficiency, high direct labor variance, and low production. During such times, the supervisory organization also needs to be expanded, and experienced trainers make up one of the principal sources of supervision. If the executive waits until the last minute to secure trainers, he probably will find none available. Waiting until the last minute to hire trainees may force the executive to forgo certain basic qualifications, compounding the difficulty.

Response to probable effects depends upon the executive's views, satisfactions, and his ability to evaluate. Responses may be enthusiastic, aggressive, constructive, or effective. On the other hand, they may be unthinking, lukewarm, or even defensive.

Even when logical persuasion is preceded by conditioning steps, people are typically more concerned about how a proposition will affect them than they are about the general merits of the proposition. The executive must translate these basic quality points into benefits that will be received by the individual beneficiary or the working group. In the unification of views these benefits and losses should be carefully outlined before introducing them for consideration. People do respond favorably to such benefits. They are fundamental stimuli to constructive thought and action. The executive aims to generate this responsiveness to the situation by unification of views.

An American Management Association booklet on "Motivation," Series 155, comments that "People seek to achieve a sense of importance from doing difficult but important tasks which help implement goals which they or their friends seek." This may be true, but it is sometimes difficult to reconcile with the nonresponsive individual who, visualizing the company as an indestructible institution, cultivates a negative attitude. The statement, "We will have a lot of trouble if we try to make this method work" has been made in dozens of different instances.

Frequently, evident facts are not the basic cause of noncooperation. The noncooperating individual usually blames something (generally fixed conditions) or someone other than himself for his failure. Failure to respond is also indicated when he becomes pugnacious, when he tries to "make something" out of it, and when he does not accept responsibility for his factual or logical position.

Only when executive response is positive and constructive can general cooperation be secured to keep the company advancing. For an effective, lasting response, executives need to give valid, intelligent evaluations to the probable effects.

V 6–3: *Rely on Convictions*

Convictions are substantial beliefs in the likelihood of an expected happening or in the validity of an adopted position. Until now, a flexible executive attitude has been encouraged. Now, upon determining the official position, reservations are dropped and faith in the final conclusion strengthens the executive's attitude.

This point in the executive cycle can be compared to concrete. When first poured, concrete is relatively easy to move for conduits and reinforcing steel, but when set, the difficulty in moving is multiplied many times. In the same manner, the optimum firmness of views as to certainty becomes more rigid during the item's development in consideration depth. The executive is now ready to rely upon faith in his associates' capabilities. He will release concern for the validity of the official position. Each individual is unquestionably assured of success of the unified position.

Executives work in a field of undetermined certainties, and risks are frequent. Judgment and courage are desirable. The certainty that a determined plan will produce results is an important consideration. Uncertainty or insecurity, on the other hand, may retard decision and advancement. Justified convictions in the effectiveness of alternatives, approaches, and techniques overcome uncertainty or hesitancy and permit progressive operations that will produce results.

It may be overemphasizing the obvious to say that executives who can be relied upon, whose statements have reliability, and whose actions lead into results, are likely to be successful. These qualifications in an executive indicate character. Character is a sum of traits conferring distinctiveness—a stamp of individuality upon a person impressed by nature, education, or habit. It permits another individual to act upon that person's advice with a clear conscience and, in fact, to rely upon his convictions.

People like to deal with persons of character, whom they can trust and with whom they have a relation of mutual confidence and certainty. Loyalty and morale within an organization are closely relevant to this point. Sincerity and other character traits play a substantial part in dealing with certainty. An effectively cooperating management team has no occasion for mutual distrust. Unwavering faith and trust in a fellow executive are invaluable teamwork characteristics. The heart of executive work is getting things done by others while shouldering responsibility for successful completion.

V 6–4: Desire Advantages

Confidence that an undertaking is performable is naturally desirable. Many times success is gained, however, when there has been little previous indication of success. All that has confronted the executive has been discouragement. It is, therefore, a great stimulus to executive accomplishment if the consequences of effective operations are fully understood. Executives need to build an earnest and commendable aspiration for advantages which become the constructive conditions of success.

Advantages are particular conditions of superiority existing in relation to comparable conditions in other instances or situations. Competitive advantages today may become disadvantages tomorrow because of the consistent progress of competitors.

People do things for benefits. Executives should agree that the undertaking should benefit the individual as well as the organization. All concerned should desire expected advantages from that undertaking. They need to seek and enter into the quest for promised incentives with positive enthusiasm. This applies to the broad scope of a career in addition to the immediate problem. Sometimes, the personal desires of comfort, prestige, and leisure are greater than the desire to advance the item.

Also, the advantages desired by certain members of the group often conflict with others. Such situations call for a clear statement of the mutual advantages the group seeks.

Executives must firmly believe that the advantages of impending events will be favorable.

EVALUATING SATISFACTIONS: DETERMINE PLANS

P 6–1: Find Criteria

Criteria are characteristics or qualities common to things being evaluated. They are taken into consideration when conclusions are reached, constituting the grounds or standards of evaluation. Criteria of evaluation frequently need to be found. Therefore, executives search for useful operating material and arrange it in definite orderly form. If not predetermined, the basis of the arrangement underlying their decisions may then be sought. Thus, they ascertain the criteria, whether they do it before or after evaluation.

Often it is possible to decide the basis for ranking or evaluating something before the actual process. Determining the basis before ranking, however, can be a ponderous impediment. If the executive delegates ranking to others, then it is usually desirable to find and communicate the criteria by which the evaluation should be done.

The decision-making process often consists of a series of small decisions within the problem area rather than one single, large decision. Small decisions may furnish the material for an important decision. An orderly list of projected views, actions, and results may suggest clues leading to early determination. The practice of occupying oneself with smaller decisions, even though the practice commonly advances the item, may lead to overlooking the importance of a major decision. Even though it is of a broad and fundamental scope, the major decision may be obscured in the stream of small decisions in which it appears.

P 6–2: Rank Selections

So that matters undertaken for the day may be scheduled in sequence, priority must be established. When such an evaluation is undertaken, the executive usually finds that many high-priority items are competing with each other for his time and effort.

In collecting content elements executives may visualize each element as having the same value. They then maintain a random perspective undistracted by evaluation.

Before ranking, the executive must select the elements to be ranked. These selected elements may be areas of opportunity, alternatives, or persons. In ranking selections, two or more subjects are arranged in order of usefulness. Each element has its own relative usefulness to the plan, and each is affected by importance, urgency, availability, or suitability for execution. A common activity in executive operations is selection and elimination so that the executive may determine priority in his undertakings.

Ranking involves a forced choice, even though choosing between unlike entries may be inconvenient. Rating differs in that it usually assigns a level of value rather than a relative order of value.

In ranking selections, parts of a situation may be evaluated in terms of relative satisfaction to a standard. Individuals are frequently ranked at Williamson-Dickie to measure relative performance. Division sales managers not only rank salesmen, but also write descriptive reports of each salesman's performance. This descriptive report is of great value in evaluating a salesman's performance, substantiating the rankings.

Another evaluation procedure is useful when evaluating a large number of elements, say from 10 to 36. The procedure involves first pairing off the odd-numbered selections against the even-numbered ones and then successively selecting the survivor of each pairing. In this way the top alternative element of each cycle of pairing comes to the peak of the pyramid quickly. The last remaining element then becomes Number 1 in the ranking. This procedure is illustrated in the exhibit that follows.

FIGURE 8.

EOT EVALUATION PROCEDURE

STEPS	KEY POINTS

1   Arrange the elements in simple, alphabetical or numerical order.

   11   Designate symbol to identify if necessary.

   12   List selected elements on left side of form, leaving space for as many columns as rankings or cycles may be needed.

STEPS | KEY POINTS

2 First Cycle

21 Pair off listed elements, giving a value of 1 for the more important in each pair and 2 for the second in importance in each pair. Write rank numbers in first column.

2101 When a single numbered element remains, assign rank of o and pair off with remaining odd number when it can be paired.

22 Pair off remaining elements, valued 1, giving a value of 1 for the more important and 2 for the second in importance.

23 Continue pairing off elements valued 1 until only one element remains with a value of 1.

2301 Always evaluate "o" elements.

24 Assign Rank #1 to this element and discontinue evaluating it on subsequent cycles.

2401 Draw line across balance of columns not used for this element.

3 Second Cycle

31 Copy first evaluation figures entered in first cycle by pairs until last ranked (at Step 24) element appears.

3101 Use only the first value stated on the left side of the element.

32 Starting with first element now remaining after last ranked element excluded, pair off balance of elements and again place value of 1 or 2 as described above.

3201 A different pairing will always appear from this point.

33 Continue placing values of 1 or 2 by pairs of elements valued until only one element remains with a value of 1, as at Step 24.

STEPS	KEY POINTS

34 Rank the element which survives from the second cycle, No. 2, and discontinue evaluating it on subsequent cycles, as provided in Step 24.

4   Third Cycle

41 Proceed as in the second cycle until Rank #3 is determined.

5   Repeat the evaluation by column until all desired numbers of elements are evaluated.

6   List elements in order of rank.

NOTE: This procedure is incomplete as to the 100% utilization of previous pairings, and the elimination of duplication has not been provided for in the procedure. Application of the procedure will yield clues to simplified use.

P 6–3: *Authorize Decisions*

Executives joining in the activity of determination should now reach a state of subjective satisfaction and resolution. At this concluding point, the plan or pattern takes on a definiteness in which previously considered alternatives are discarded from consideration, and the adopted course is reinforced by conviction and decisiveness. Thus, the direction of future conduct with regard to the item in question is set.

A *decision* is reached when the executive arrives at the state of mind in which one particular alternative has been definitely selected for action from those before him, and a cycle of action based on the decision is imminent or permissible. A decision is a plan with the quality of certainty as a major consideration. A mere hope or wish is not a decision, because a decision, to be effective, must be performable and must be backed by a determination.

A decision should be structured at the start with a flexible hand, so the firmness can be crystallized by degrees as the pattern fits into place. Once settled, a decision should be held firmly. The executive, after repeated experience with operating techniques, learns to make rigid decisions.

Decisions are susceptible to fragmentation and selectivity, as are other executive activities. Some situations require the executive to decide on the first part as conditions permit and not allow concern about the last part to delay the first decision. Frequently, decisions visualized as a single point emerge as a series of decisions or a plan of operations.

A function of the senior executive is to authorize decisions. The decisions, which permit action to be resumed or continued, frequently are based on precedent and policy. To *authorize* is to pass final decision upon a plan, to approve, to sanction, and to empower so that action may be produced within the designated powers and duties of an organization.

Authority is a conferred power implying the right to act, to command, to make final decisions, and to enforce them. It also involves delegating subordinate authority and influencing the conduct and actions of others within the limits of jurisdiction.

Sometimes authorizing decisions is unpleasant, but this does not excuse the executive of responsibility to attempt to decide something about a valid problem. Many times progress is blocked by indecision and lack of self-reliance. Sometimes executives procrastinate, demur, or vacillate, and advancement is suspended. Sometimes the delay is deliberate in order to permit a tentative decision to age or mature; but such a justification easily may be used to rationalize an indecisive attitude.

Frequently the executive is faced with the alternative of deciding with possibly poor judgment and incomplete information, or not deciding at all. In the writer's experience, more executives err on the side of not deciding at all rather than deciding with poor judgment.

Evidence of the decisiveness of executives may be simply revealed by asking their juniors to list the items on which they are awaiting decisions. This should quickly reveal opportunities to authorize decisions. Whether an executive fails to use his authority to decide or whether he exceeds his authority in making decisions, are defects in decision making which must be eliminated for effective teamwork in an organization. The goal of an effective working group should be to make a firm decision, soundly based, and to stick to it under all reasonable circumstances.

P 6–4: Release Agreements

At this point an agreement should be implied or committed. If there have been no undue reservations or disagreements, the item should be released for the expected advancement effort. It is presupposed that assignments have been wholeheartedly accepted, that everyone agrees on the item's status, and that the next step is definite enough to provide accountability.

There is an intention and expectancy of action, and the assignment of the next step is released and sent on its way. The senior executive suspends his direct participation, and the junior gives or implies assurance that he will handle this matter and report to the senior. The executive group as well as the reviewing chairman should expect effort and good faith to be applied behind the agreed next steps. If there is any modification of plans or assignments, it is the participating executives' responsibility to communicate with their associates in advance so that full agreement on the new course of action may be maintained.

What happens after the release? Any uncertainty in the senior's assignment may cause misinterpretation, loss of time, interference, or even opposition. On the other hand, the senior should ascertain and correctly express the action he expects. This starts implementation of the plan and the developing of means for the junior to get it into action. The cost of repeat assignments is great, and both junior and senior need to share the responsibility for preventing it.

EVALUATING SATISFACTIONS: PRODUCE ACTIONS

A 6–1: Handle Noncompletions

Uncompleted work tasks are accumulated obligations which require disposition in line with an executive's responsibility. They are jobs or undertaken items that the executive has not found time to complete. They may be in the form of unread mail or reports, unanswered letters, unconsidered problems, or undecided issues.

Many executives stay behind in their work to a degree, because all can think of more things they must do. These tasks weigh upon their minds and, if excessive, can interfere with the spirit which induces action. Catching up on uncompleted work tasks clears the deck for action, giving a feeling of reserve time. A foreseen lack of time may retard the ability to concentrate upon an undertaking. Executives frequently must decide whether to spend time on the immediate, pressing necessities of their work, or to spend time on items of long-term value.

It is beneficial to cultivate the habit of completing as many details as possible on each item scheduled. The more details handled that are well in advance of the due date, the greater is the certainty of item completion.

A 6–2: *Moderate Refinement Extremes*

A *refinement extreme* is the excessive development of any single factor within a situation. It is an extreme of stress, improvement, or purification, and may result in oversubtleties or vague distinctions. These extremes must often be moderated to keep them in proper bounds without being excessive or deficient in degree. Extreme factors arising in a situation must be adjusted to accommodate the needs of persons, time, and situation itself.

The executive frequently must decide whether to spend additional time and effort refining the present course of action or shift to another area that may prove more productive. There is generally an optimal point where underrefinement stops and overrefinement begins. At this point such considerations as satisfaction, certainty, and cost should be balanced. Overrefinement at one time does not mean that desirability for later refinement is unnecessary. Overrefinement at this stage may cause quibbling over minutiae, which does not contribute substantially to the advancement of the item.

The intensive effort in overrefinement may be applied more productively in other areas. Time and energy must be spent to unravel extremes of overrefinement to get the item back to a workable basis. Executives frequently should settle for an approximate figure when an exact figure is not available. This permits the action to advance, while getting the actual figure may cause considerable delay. The caution, "Do not try to get the last cent of profit" is another example of balancing refinement extremes.

Sometimes overrefinement or underrefinement is caused from defects in identifying or centering on the target. Other times it arises when an individual prefers not to work on the agreed next step.

A 6–3: *Reprocess Inadequacies*

The senior executive sometimes opens conferences with the expectancy that the item is farther along in the advancement cycle than developments prove it to be. On the other hand, he may feel that the results thus far are not sufficiently adequate to warrant going on. In such cases it is necessary to reprocess the inadequate performance before proceeding further. Perhaps other executives involved in the item have not realized that until these inadequacies are acknowledged and properly handled, the item will not advance.

Inadequacies are completions which do not measure up to requirements. An inadequacy is, in fact, a defective performance, and is the opposite of what the executive was expected to attain; namely, adequacies, completions, or realizations. In *reprocessing* inadequacies the executive may repeat the application of a particular method or treatment, and reconstruct, repair, or rehandle the performance under consideration.

The executive must reprocess inadequacies when he finds modifications in the plan which do not seem to be justified by the requirements of the situation or the difficulties involved. Many times inadequacies must be reprocessed, even though the responsible executive has made a sincere effort to handle them properly. In other cases the reprocessing may have been avoidable. These unnecessary repetitions are great consumers of time and energy and may lead to unpleasant repeated assignments.

If the item is adequately handled upon reprocessing, the initial defect was probably caused by misidentification or misunderstanding. Reprocessing that is carelessly handled, on the other hand, may reveal noncooperation.

A 6–4: *Report Accomplishments*

Accomplishments are steps or intentions which have been completed or achieved. These attainments, achievements, or performances need to be reported in an objective way, whether the results are favorable or unfavorable.

The responsible executive must advise his senior executive that he is ready to report accomplishments of an item so that they can take the item into a review of results. Emphasis at this phase is not necessarily on the fact that accomplishment has been achieved at the end of the action cycle. The consideration here is that the reporting executive's cycle of action is not complete until he has reported it, even though ordinarily the senior executive also takes the responsibility of keeping himself advised by inquiry and observation.

The executive, of course, gets more satisfaction from reporting advancement than from reporting no advancement. Regardless of its nature, however, the result of this action step should be reported. The executive should not conceal, misrepresent, or merely imply any developments which have been revealed in the action cycle. This may be information essential to the advancement of the item.

If an executive has received an assignment to produce action, it is not proper for him to decide that further advancement is impossible. Circumstances may indicate that the item should be abandoned; but before it is abandoned, a full report of the failure or nonadvancement should be made.

It might be assumed that the executive should assign the entire item to the junior and expect him to handle it without reporting further until the entire item is complete. Experience has proved that, if this is done, the junior often may go so far afield that all his effort is wasted. One reason is that frequently the objective is not sufficiently identified, as in the case of many developmental items.

EVALUATING SATISFACTIONS: REVIEW RESULTS

R 6–1: *Weigh Improvements*

Improvements are increases in usefulness or value such as betterments or refinements. Opposites are impairments, deteriorations, or damages. Improvements are changes which place a situation or item in a more favorable status with respect to a desired goal.

Executives sometimes mistake mere changes as improvement. For this reason it is necessary to determine objectively if any improvement is evident and, if so, to what extent. Even though these improvements cannot always be mathematically weighed, the executive should determine the relative degree to which they satisfy the results desired for the item or situation.

Occasionally, changes result in substantial deterioration, and the situation worsens steadily. The executive must then apply his influence to the situation, seeking improvements of significant weight and effect. In doing so, he must carefully guard against viewing all improvements as equal in importance, for some will have far greater impact than others. Those improvements which promise significant consequences deserve the executive's fullest attention, of course, but he must not accept other improvements that fall far short of their potential influence.

Some elements in a situation may not be nearly so bad as they once were. But the reviewing executive's standards of satisfaction should not allow him to accept small improvements when greater ones are still possible. As he reviews results, the competent executive will constantly be weighing the improvements he sees. As he does so, he will cull unsatisfactory improvements from those in which he can safely suspend his influence.

R 6–2: Reevaluate Techniques

Techniques are carefully developed methods of performing an operating activity. In other words, they are skills, approaches, or systems which are valuable or useful in proportion to their soundness of conception and their exposure to frequent and long-time use.

To *reevaluate* is to determine again, after experience, the usefulness or importance of something; in other words, to reappraise, reexamine, or rejudge. Before experience with it, a technique may have been prejudged, and as the item changes through experience there will doubtless occur necessities and opportunities for changes in techniques. It is now possible to reevaluate it. Many techniques exist for use in item advancement and executive consideration. If accomplishments are not satisfactory, and if prospects for results are not favorable, the executive may conclude that his techniques need reevaluation. Often, he needs to diagnose his approach once again. Under any circumstances, his job is to continue making progress in the area of his own executive operations techniques.

Techniques also require an intelligent understanding of the way they are used. Some new or untried techniques have potential value, and the matter of understanding and using them is essential to productive accomplishment.

R 6–3: Suspend Influences

The executive is now faced with a decision regarding the situation. He must decide whether to pursue any remaining possibilities further. If the item status is satisfactory, his future influence in the advancement effort may be suspended, allowing him to apply his time and effort to other pressing matters.

The executive is confronted with the degree to which he wishes to participate. He considers for further attention and action the projects and the tangible operating material before him. At this point his function is to balance the certainty and risk of continuing efforts with their possible results and advantages in operations, as opposed to his suspending or withdrawing his direct influence upon the item. This will be a calculated risk.

Most of the guide points in the EOT Chart call for the executive to do something or to expend energy. His emphasis now is upon coasting and judicious neglect. There are things which make no demand upon his time and energy, and may only involve "waiting them out." Economy of executive effort ranges from working himself, as successful executives normally do in early life; then working others; and finally, working money. This move in the direction of nonparticipation, except in the case of useful necessity, is also illustrated in the shift in organizational thinking from responsibility centers to profit centers, the profit performance being the ultimate responsibility of the executive.

R 6–4: Feed Back Cycles

As the executive surveys the consequences at the end of the cycle, he must decide whether to transmit his attention to a new item or to reapply the full cycle of EOT treatment to the item currently under review. If he decides on the latter course, he will continue to direct influence upon the item and carry over things known which were disclosed in the previous advancement efforts. Then the same facts developed in reviewing results will become conditions in the new cycle and will be fed back as conditions.

A *cycle* is a series of changes to be experienced by a situation. EOT endeavors to visualize these changes as being executed in orderly sequence so that a technique or advancement sequence periodically returns to the original starting point. This operation is visualized as a circuit or circle rather than as a single consideration, guide point, or technique.

To *feed back* is to reuse a series of steps previously applied—to repeat or reenact. In feeding back, it must be borne in mind that the executive is visualizing the feeding back of a segment of operating material or situation into this advancement cycle. He is also feeding back forms of suggested effort or reminders as he deals with each segment of operating material.

This feeding back of the new cycle generally consists of attempts to advance a situation further, utilizing the particulars learned from the advancement cycle just experienced.

Cycles selected for feed-back have a varied range of scope and require different time spans. The scope or radius of the new cycle is a significant starting condition of success or failure in controlling the certainty of a new cycle. In applying operating techniques, the cycles concerning the executive vary in length according to the scope of his current operation.

As the advancement of the general item proceeds, the executive "spins off" his efforts into smaller segments of the undertaking. The techniques within the EOT Pattern may then be applied to each separate scope or separate segment of the undertaking. In this way the broad item may still be in the exposing conditions step, whereas a very small segment of the broad item may have been completed and checked off to the satisfaction of the executive evaluating the process.

Discussion of guide points has, of necessity, proceeded one word at a time; whereas, in reality, an executive may have all these considerations in mind at once. If he is not thinking of them at the same time, he, at least, is aware of their interdependence. In the following chapter effort is made to convey the simultaneous aspect of the consideration processes at each advancement step by reference to specific situations.

X

The Management Case
In Executive Development

Every large enterprise depends upon an executive development program of some kind, each program having diverse
features and existing in varying degrees of formality. Most
executives will agree, however, that the success and growth
of the enterprise depends on the growth in quality and
ability of its managers.

If executive operations are a distinct, unique kind of work,
techniques of executive operations can be learned and
taught. Efficient learning of these techniques cannot be
entrusted solely to experience, however, if the executives
of an enterprise are to develop themselves into mature,
capable leaders. Comprehensive and continuous as it must
be, executive development must receive specific and formal
attention from executives charged with the total responsibility for the enterprise. In addition, managers at all
levels must aid in fostering the proper climate for executive development.

At Williamson-Dickie, the formal and informal aspects of its executive development program have altered significantly over the past twenty years. But throughout that time period, two features have remained central to the program: (1) group participation in theoretical analysis of executive operating techniques, and (2) group study of real business situations drawn both from outside sources and the inner workings of the firm.

Formal Practice Sessions

Williamson-Dickie instituted formal practice sessions in executive operating techniques about twenty years ago. Since that time members of the executive group have met together during working hours or in the evenings to discuss company problems and similar matters. These sessions have been aimed not at solving a specific problem or at solutions themselves but at improved methods of seeking solutions.

As early as 1942 we began a weekly series of evening meetings with 12 to 15 of the firm's top executives, testing by discussion and application to actual situations the logical soundness of our Performance Factors, then 21 in number. After a thorough revision of the EOT pattern, and reduction in the number of factors to 12, another series of meetings was begun in 1949. Attending were only six executives, all at the vice-president level or higher. These Top Management Conferences, as they were called, concentrated upon the executive operating system. The theoretical framework was closely hitched to the problems arising in the day-to-day operations of the business. These early efforts strived for an optimum combination of theoretical discussion and actual business particulars. Such a combination of theory and practice has continued to underlie the practice sessions through which our executives gain ability and confidence. New practical situations reinforce the general theory.

In 1950, all department heads began attending Saturday morning practice sessions. Later in the decade, several of their supervisory assistants and staff specialists were added to the EOT group. By 1960, almost every company executive had participated in the EOT sessions.

So that they can be carefully analyzed, EOT Conferences are usually recorded, and transcripts are later supplied to all participants. More than 50,000 pages of such transcripts have accumulated since the inception of the program. Careful analysis of the transcripts has provided a basis for improvement of the instructional techniques and the theoretical framework. Also, the transcripts can be used to measure the progress, understanding, and participation of each of the executives in the conference.

Use of Case Material

The development of the EOT Pattern has been marked by a distinctively inductive approach, and the use of case materials drawn from actual business situations has been an important feature of the system since its inception.

At first, the effort to broaden perspective led to conscious study and analysis of the behavior of executives in other firms. A number of these executives were questioned at length about their approach to management activities. This effort, incidentally, started the collection of questions asked by executives.

These questions were carefully analyzed for clues to successful executive action. After the generalizations were extracted, the facts in the situation were often used to illustrate the principles, performance factors, or guide points. Actual business problems or cases have provided insights into executive operating techniques while also serving to illustrate generalizations.

Most of the early cases were necessarily drawn from individual experiences of executives in Williamson-Dickie, and each case related directly to one department's operations. While these cases were effective in themselves, their scope was somewhat too narrow and restrictive to permit generalization about *all* types of executive activity. To find a universal pattern of executive activity and to connect this pattern with all types of business, each participant had to broaden his perspective considerably.

These executives eventually developed a procedure whereby the elements or particulars of the cases being analyzed could be classified according to guide point. This procedure specifically pinpoints the type of excutive activity exemplified in the case in analyzing not only what happened but in discovering how and why failures occurred.

To supplement the scant supply of cases, Professor Towl recommended study of the vast number of cases in the growing library of the Harvard Graduate School of Business, suggesting that they might provide us with the insights and illustrations we desired. This case library contained a treasure of illustrations well-suited to our analytical purposes.

Not all of the cases in the Harvard library, however, lent themselves well to EOT analysis and discussion. Many were apparently designed to induce familiarity with the technical details of certain business procedures. From among the thousands available, cases had to be chosen that concentrated primarily upon the administrative and supervisory practices of executives.

By deriving the guide points of EOT from these "business cases," an attempt was made to avoid excessive and unreal theorizing. Rather than stating categorically what an executive *should* do, EOT attempts to discover and point out the way that successful executives typically think and act. It was recognized that executives often act intuitively and are at a loss to explain just what they have done. Nevertheless, their operations can be seen to fit into the pattern of executive behavior outlined in this volume.

In EOT Conferences, the participants were able to classify the elements or events in a case according to the logical outlines of advancement steps and executive considerations. This classification process, it was found, facilitated analysis and discussion of the case by providing a common language to identify executive thoughts and actions. The conference leader might ask, "What was this executive doing (or considering) at this point?" Participants could usually agree that the executive was, for example, clarifying a misunderstanding, or authorizing a decision. In a similar manner, participants could detect when an essential advancement step had been overlooked or when the executive had failed to consider the situation in sufficient depth.

Cases particularly sought were those written for group analysis of developments and actions taken step by step. Cases were desired that would also lead participants to diagnose the situation and develop judgment in designing a course of action. Among the best cases for this purpose were those that presented only the particulars in a situation, leaving the necessity and responsibility for problem definition and decision-making to the participants. Even those cases that fell short of these criteria, however, could be analyzed and discussed within the EOT pattern.

Homework Assignments

Almost every executive development program provides for directed study on the executive's own time. This study may be directed into a wide variety of reading areas. Sometimes it is intended to broaden the executive's cultural outlook; more often it is aimed at increasing the executive's technical competence. Broad-gauge study programs are aimed at both objectives.

In the Williamson-Dickie executive development program, the broader aspects of each executive's awareness are not overlooked; but concentrated group study and activity are aimed at understanding of the management process. This requires study of executive operating techniques and, at the same time, application of these techniques to problems exposed by management cases. Guided by tested procedures for case analysis, participants in the EOT program study a variety of cases. In addition, they prepare and present cases drawn from their own personal experiences.

Procedures for analysis of cases are constantly undergoing revision and improvement. Still, it may be instructive to note the systematic analytical technique in use in 1961. Later developments, of course, may further enhance its usefulness.

Case Content Elements or Particulars

In every situation, certain events or developments are more significant than others. In legal practice, the lawyer briefs a case by summarizing the facts leading up to a court decision. In EOT analysis of management cases, a similar briefing procedure is followed that cuts through extraneous or less important developments in the case. In this way, the most elemental particulars in the case are summarized. These summarized facts are termed *content particulars* or *content elements*. Together, and in sequence, the particulars form an outline of the case.

The first step in case analysis is to read the case carefully, underlining those portions considered most significant. The underlined portions are then transferred to an "alphabet sheet," a single page on which the content elements are entered beside the letter that begins the first word of the sentence. In the transfer, wording of the content particular is simplified and abstracted into terse language that is almost telegraphic.

After the particulars of the case are written on the alphabet sheet, they are numbered to indicate their sequence in the unfolding of the case. If the case analyst decides to insert additional elements, he may indicate their sequence by labeling them; for example, "3A" and "3B." Sequencing the content particulars thus enables the analyst to relate the facts in the case in their proper order.

Classifying Particulars by Guide Points

The next step in the analysis is classification of the particulars according to the most applicable guide point. From among the 144 guide points, the analyst selects one, two, or three that most precisely describe the thoughts or actions of the people involved in the case.

Classifying particulars by guide points often requires the analyst to assume an executive point of view toward the case situation. In some cases, classification will proceed as if the analyst were a top manager in the organization—all-seeing, all-knowing, and all-powerful. This might be called the omnipotent point of view. At times, the analyst will adopt the role and status of one of the principal characters involved in the case, and he will classify particulars according to this restrictive point of view.

In deciding upon the proper guide point classification, the analyst may wish to pose questions such as these:

"What is the purpose of this supervisor's action?"

"What was this supervisor doing, in a managerial sense?"

"What guide point did this executive follow at this point?"

Occasionally, the particular is classified in a negative way, with the guide point illustrating failure of an executive to accomplish some desirable step, consideration, or guide point.

Classifying the case particulars is an exacting task. It requires intimate knowledge of the 144 guide points and their concrete referents.

Similarity of EOT Guide Points to Musical Notation

Continued experience since 1946 with Executive Operations Techniques has indicated there may be a useful analogy between the intuitively felt guide points with which executives work and musical notes. Just as there is a sense of harmony, there is also a central sense which comes into play involving awareness of and discrimination between elements of useful material.

Just as the elements of musical harmony or discord may be isolated by identifying the component notes, the elements of harmony or inconsistency in an executive situation may be isolated. Music involves a "sixth sense" which permits two or more notes to be played simultaneously without causing dissonance. In the same way two or more EOT guide points may appear in the same situation at the same time without causing item impairment. Both are subject to changes in sequence, emphasis, range, or key, depending upon the conditions or the effect desired.

The growth in mastering the guide points also may be similar to developing an ear for music. The participant must first learn to follow a piece exactly as it is written by note before he can begin improvising. Improvisation is what gives either activity interest, novelty, and the opportunity for creative effect. Although there is a great deal of similarity in different renditions of the same piece, the points of similarity fade out of the picture and become incidental to the narrowed range of refinement wherein this creative accomplishment of separate musicians is occurring. Williamson-Dickie executives are striving to set up these "musical notes" so that when they hear and recognize them in a situation, they can say, "Of course, that is *declaring standards,*" or "that is *detecting trends,*" or "*observing evidence.*"

As in music, there also is a distinction between "appreciation" and "performance." If notes and musical compositions differ, there is also a difference between the 144 guide points and the approaches executives use. "Chopsticks" and Beethoven's "Ninth Symphony" were both composed with the same musical notations. Either mediocre or outstanding executive operations may go on record and the same identifying symbols will have been used in each.

The musical analogy might be further extended in visualizing the executive as the conductor of a group of musicians who share a common system of notes as a system of coordination. Just as the creative art of the musician cannot be imposed from the outside, so insight into the use of an EOT must come from within the individual executive. He must identify himself with the use of these techniques. The individual who hopes to gain skill must have an internal urge—the urge to understand how to become a better executive. This skill may be clarified by case application, experience, and discrimination among the guide points in actual use.

Undertaking Items in the Case

Many of the cases selected for EOT analysis present the facts in a problem situation but do not attempt to define a solution. With such a case, participants outline the items they would undertake in developing a successful conclusion to the case. As stated in previous discussion, an item is a unit of executive work to be scheduled and handled by the executive. Participants are asked to carve from the fact situation, summarized by the content particulars, those "things to do" which can be reduced to action status.

Some cases, of course, present a complete narrative of an administrative incident and make no attempt to claim that the events represent

either effective or ineffective handling. Their primary purpose is to provoke discussion. These cases can also be analyzed within the EOT
procedure, of course, and items can be undertaken as they might arise
from the stress points revealed in the case.

Items are usually worded in laconic language, using noun phrases as
much as possible since verbs are more subject to altered connotation
as the item progresses. Like the content particulars, items are listed on
a separate alphabet sheet. They are then ranked according to order of
importance, usefulness, or the chronological sequence in which they
must be carried out. Rank order is indicated by an encircled number
alongside the item.

To preserve continuity with the particulars, the items may be "indexed"
to the portions of the case situation which provoked undertaking that
item. Indexing can be indicated by encircling the sequence number of
the particular or particulars underneath the item wording.

Because items will vary in scope from narrow to broad, it may be
necessary to delineate "next steps" under the broader items to show
more precisely and specifically what the executive must do to complete
his task. Next steps are usually designated as A-1's, A-2's, A-3's, etc. More
than items, next steps are phrased with action verbs.

Items are also classified by guide points in a manner similar to the
classification of the content particulars. Items must be performable
within the reference frame of the executive to whom they are assigned.
In deciding upon the guide points most aptly describing the executive
operating technique emphasized in the selected item, the analyst will
often seek to answer a question such as this:

"What should I do if I were a responsible executive in this case
situation?"

With the creation, indexing, ranking, and classification of the items,
the case analysis is largely complete.

An EOT Case Conference

In the EOT Case Conference, each individual analysis is combined
with all the others in an attempt to arrive at the group's consensus.
This combination is secured through informal discussions within sub-
committees and recorded discussions involving the whole group of conferences. Participation among the executives in the group is encouraged;
each executive is given an opportunity to state his views.

The main purpose of the case conference is not simply agreement upon the proper methods of handling the problems posed by the case under discussion. Instead, the objective is more complete understanding of executive operating techniques and of the guide points that constitute an executive's "kit of tools."

When an executive group is just beginning to become familiar with EOT analysis, processing a case through a conference will require a great deal of time. Before the group has acquired skill in selecting guide points and mastering the mechanical procedures, additional conferences may be necessary to decide upon wording and classification of the content elements or particulars and to undertake the items arising from the case. With practice and experience in the method, however, the time required is reduced until an entire case can be covered adequately in a two- or three-hour session.